SOLOMON CARTER FULLER

Where My Caravan Has Rested

Mary Kaplan

University Press of America,® Inc.
Lanham · Boulder · New York · Toronto · Oxford

Library of Congress Control Number: 2005929564
ISBN 0-7618-3265-3 (paperback : alk. ppr.)

Contents

List of Illustrations   v

Foreword   vii

Preface   ix

Acknowledgments   xi

Introduction: Fuller's Arrival in Germany, 1905   xiii

1. The Beginning: John Lewis Fuller, Norfolk, Virginia, 1830   1

2. A New Life in Africa: Monrovia, 1852   7

3. In Pursuit of a Dream: North Carolina, 1889   15

4. Learning and Teaching: Boston, 1897   21

5. The Science of Germany: Munich, 1904   33

6. The Doctor and the Sculptor: Westboro, 1906   41

7. Pioneer in American Psychiatry: Framingham, 1909   49

8. Contributions to Science and Medicine: Westborough, 1911   55

9. The Later Years: Framingham, 1933   67

10. Recognition of Accomplishments: Boston, 1974   79

Epilogue: Washington, D.C., 2001   83

Appendix: Publications of Solomon Carter Fuller   85

Notes   87

Index   99

About the Author   105

List of Illustrations

Cover. Courtesy of the Boston University Alumni Medical Library Archives.
1. Anna Ursala James Fuller. Courtesy of Solomon Carter Fuller, Jr. and John Lewis Fuller.
2. Solomon Carter Fuller. Courtesy of Solomon Carter Fuller, Jr. and John Lewis Fuller.
3. Westboro Insane Hospital. Courtesy of Westborough State Hospital.
4. Psychiatric clinic at the Ludwig-Maximilians University, Munich, Germany, 1904. Courtesy of Klinik for Psychiatrie and Psychotherapie, Klinikum d. Universitat Muchen.
5. Dr. Alois Alzheimer and students in Alzheimer's laboratory (Fuller is seated to the left of Alzheimer), 1905. Courtesy of Solomon Carter Fuller, Jr. and John Lewis Fuller.
6. Letter to Fuller from Paul Ehrlich confirming arrangements for Fuller to carry mice from Prof. Ehrlich's laboratory to the United States to be used for research, 1905. Courtesy of Solomon Carter Fuller, Jr. and John Lewis Fuller.
7. Solomon Carter Fuller. Courtesy of Solomon Carter Fuller, Jr. and John Lewis Fuller.
8. Mary (May) Bragg Weston. Courtesy of Solomon Carter Fuller, Jr. and John Lewis Fuller.
9. Fuller (last row, far right) is among the group of scientists invited to celebrate Clark University's 20th Anniversary. Courtesy of the Clark University Archives. See next page for key to all individuals in photo.
10. Fuller family on front steps of Solomon and Meta's home in Framingham, Massachusetts, 1944. (Front row: son Solomon, Jr., grandson John, Meta, grandson Robert, daughter-in-law Marie. Second row: son Thomas, daughter-in-law Harriet, grandson Solomon III, grandson Thomas, Jr. Back row: son Perry.) Courtesy of Solomon Carter Fuller, Jr. and John Lewis Fuller.
11. Solomon and Meta. Courtesy of the Boston University Alumni Medical Library Archives.
12. Letter acknowledging Fuller's contribution to the training of medical staff at Tuskegee Institute, 1950. Courtesy of Solomon Carter Fuller, Jr. and John Lewis Fuller.
13. The Dr. Solomon Fuller Mental Health Center, Boston. Courtesy of the Dr. Solomon Carter Fuller Mental Health Center, Boston.
14. *Boston Sunday Globe* cartoon featuring Fuller, 1976. Courtesy of the *Boston Sunday Globe*, May 9, 1976.
15. Invitation to the dedication of the Fuller Middle School, 1995. Courtesy of the family of Solomon Carter Fuller.
16. Solomon Carter Fuller, Jr. and his second wife, Grace. Photo by Mary Kaplan.

1. Franz Boas
2. E.B. Titchener
3. William James
4. William Stern
5. Leo Burgerstein
6. G. Stanley Hall
7. Sigmund Freud
8. Carl G. Jung
9. Adolf Meyer
10. H.S. Jennings
11. C.E. Seashore
12. Joseph Jastrow
13. J. Mck. Cattrell
14. E.F. Buchner
15. E. Katzenellenbogen
16. Ernest Jones
17. A.A. Brill
18. Wm. H. Burnham
19. A.F. Chamberlain
20. Albert Schinz
21. J.A. Magni
22. B.T. Baldwin
23. F. Lyman Wells
24. G.M. Forbes
25. E.A. Kirkpatrick
26. Sandor Ferenczi
27. E.C. Sanford
28. J.P. Porter
29. Sakyo Kanda
30. Hikoso Kakise
31. G.E. Dawson
32. S.P. Hayes
33. E.B. Holt
34. C.S. Berry
35. G.M. Whipple
36. Frank Drew
37. J.W.A. Young
38. L.N. Wilson
39. K.J. Karlson
40. H.H. Goddard
41. H.I. Klopp
42. S.C. Fuller

Foreword

Out of the huts of history's shame
I rise
Up from a past that's rooted in shame
I rise
I am a black ocean, leaping and wide,
Welling and swelling I bear in the tide.
Leaving behind nights of terror and fear
I rise
Into a daybreak that's wondrously clear
I rise
Bringing the gifts that my ancestors gave,
I am the dream and the hope of the slave.
I rise
I rise
I rise.

Maya Angelou

Where My Caravan Has Rested is a story of courage, perseverance, humility, integrity, and one man's determination to succeed against all odds. To some, this may be a story of hope, hope of achievement in the face of adversity. It traces Dr. Fuller's contribution to the field of psychiatry - an African-American, born in Liberia, West Africa, whose work spanned three continents. It tells of how he came to become the nation's first African American psychiatrist and one of the first African Americans to hold a teaching position at a medical university. It is the story of a father, a husband, a researcher, and a pioneer in mental health and neuroscience. *Where My Caravan Has Rested* is a refrain to an unsung hero.

Authoring this foreword holds much significance for me as director of the Solomon Carter Fuller Mental Health Center, a community mental health center named after Dr. Fuller. The Dr. Solomon Carter Fuller Mental Health Center is owned and operated by the Massachusetts Department of Mental Health. It provides an array of mental health services to Department of Mental Health eligible clients. It services some of the most disenfranchised and underserved residents in the Metropolitan Boston Area. Services include inpatient, case management, homeless outreach, community rehabilitation, supported education and employment, transitional shelter, community housing, and independent living.

In many ways the center carries the work of Dr. Fuller forward. In collaboration with the Boston Medical Center, the Center is a training site for psychiatry students and residents. It supports a multi-cultural psychology-training program and focuses on quality and diversity in rehabilitation services.

Like all public agencies the Center has had to overcome some fiscally challenging times. In keeping with the Fuller's spirit of resilience, the Center has been able to "weather the storm" while staying focused on delivering quality patient care. This is the kind of commitment and dedication that has come to be known at the Dr. Solomon Carter Fuller Mental Health Center. Within the pages of this book one will see that these are characteristics that embodied the man after whom the Center was named.

Dr. Fuller remained undaunted by what some may see as insurmountable in an attempt to achieve his goals. Likewise the Center has been able to live out its mission and articulate its goals and visions in very new and compelling ways and as it strives to re-design services in more efficient, creative, and innovative ways in these changing times.

In Dr. Fuller's records he stated that he did not attach any importance to what he had done. However, his contributions to Alzheimer's disease research and the evolution of American psychiatry have been significant. His research work contributed to the body of knowledge in degenerative brain disorders, Alzheimer's disease, pernicious anemia in the mentally ill, and the effects of chronic alcoholism on the brain and manic-depression.

Along the way Dr. Fuller kept record of his family's history and some of his accomplishments. He titled his story "Where My Caravan Has Rested," a title that implies a journey's end. Although this may rightly be the ending of one man's journey through life, the "Caravan" keeps moving.

The "Caravan" continues its journey along the city streets, through the back roads and into the neighborhoods of Boston ..Rising with the tide, bringing hope of rehabilitation to individuals, families and communities touched by mental illness and brain dysfunction. In Metropolitan Boston specifically at the Dr. Solomon Carter Fuller Community Mental Health Center, the spirit and purpose of Dr. Fuller lives on.

Where My Caravan Has Rested is a celebration of the life of a great man and a testament to Dr Solomon Carter Fuller's great accomplishments. It is the obstacles that one has to overcome that sometimes determine the size of his/her accomplishments. This is a story about a man who had to overcome great obstacles to reach his goal, making him a truly accomplished man.

May the dust of the "Caravan" continue to rise, *Welling and swelling as it bears in the tide.*

Mary-Louise White, M. Ed., Ph.D., RN
Center Director
Dr. Solomon Carter Fuller Mental Health Center
85 East Newton Street
Boston, MA. 02118
August 4, 2004

Preface

Prefabricated Negroes are sketched on sheets of paper and superimposed upon the Negro community; then when someone thrusts his head through the pages and yells, 'Watch out there, Jack, there's people living under here,' they are all shocked and indignant.[1]

Ralph Ellison, *Shadow and Act*

Solomon Carter Fuller: Where My Caravan Has Rested is the documentation of the life and accomplishments of an African American who would not permit the racism of the early 20th century to quench resolve and commitment to a productive life in medicine and scientific research.

Despite Dr. Fuller's personal and professional accomplishments, he has not been recognized in the annals of American black history or the history of medicine. The challenge to write about Dr. Fuller's life came in the form of a letter from my father, a retired physician and medical historian:

November 22, 1994

Dear Mary,

Since you are now becoming famous in the medical world, let me suggest you be a little (or lot) different from other "dry dust" writers. Put a little history into your efforts and works!

For example, how did a particular syndrome become named "Alzheimer's"? You will note the first three works on the subject carry only his name. His students dare not publish the hard work they did for the boss until leaving his lab, returning to their own countries.

Let's give A. some credit…e.g. for probably first noting this peculiar syndrome in his large clinic…but his unrewarded underlings who made the additional studies and did all of the histopathology etc. were never named. For example, an American working in his lab by the name of Solomon Fuller took the clinical case, studied it carefully and did subsequent histopathology studies. It was common at the end of the 19th century and up until W.W. I, for all wanting the very best graduate work in medicine to go to the then best place, Germany. Fuller was one of these. Now, you must know something of the times and how things worked. One man headed the lab and was usually famous and it was an honor to work under him… do all the work and get no credit. These hot-shot chiefs were called 'Germeinerott', literally translated as arrogant (and smelly) big cheeses. You could not question them and any suggestion you might dare to make, if reasonably potentially productive (for the chief) became his idea and his product. The scientific world would never know the truth. Some did publish their ideas and continue to carry out their projects after leaving Germany and returning home. But feeling strongly the obligation, and as was the tradition, those returning to their own country thrived on the fact that they had studied under the great and fabulous Professor Schmaltz at Warburg, etc. and soon forgot or dismissed the fact that it was they who had made ol'Schmaltzie famous.

So it was with Fuller. Alzheimer's notable works were published in and after 1907. Fuller's after that. You might stir up history and be bold enough to suggest the syndrome be called Alzheimer/Fuller syndrome...but, yet, another point...was Fuller so long unrecognized because he was black?

Happy hunting...well worth the divorce*

Love,
Dad

*Tell Roy, I'm only joking!

My original intent when I began my research on Solomon Carter Fuller was to keep from oblivion, his contributions to science and medicine, generally known only as bibliographic citations. Those contributions were described in an article that I co-authored with my father that was published in the *Journal of the History of the Neurosciences* in 2000. As I learned more about Dr. Fuller's life and family history, I realized that his life story would serve as an important contribution to our society and its history, not only for its account of a man whose achievements were many, but also for its perspectives of what it was like to be black in the days of slavery, in the colonization of Liberia, and as a physician in early twentieth century white America. During my interviews with Dr. Fuller's only surviving son, Solomon Carter, Jr., he requested that I write about his father, not only as a scientist and physician, but as a man with strong family and professional values, who had the courage to pursue his dreams despite the obstacles he encountered in a racist society. Sadly, Solomon Carter Fuller, Jr. did not live to see the completion of his father's story, passing away at the age of ninety in 2001. This book is dedicated to his memory.

Mary Kaplan
Tampa, Florida
August 2004

Acknowledgments

I am deeply grateful to those who have helped to bring to print the story of Solomon Carter Fuller's life. I am especially indebted to Dr. Fuller's family. His son, Solomon Carter Fuller, Jr. and daughter-in-law, Grace Fuller (both deceased) welcomed me into their home in Cape Cod, where I spent many hours listening to stories about Dr. Fuller. Toward the end of Solomon, Jr.'s life, the couple had moved to Framingham to be near their family. During my last visit, several months before his death, he was very frail and unable to engage in a conversation. Despite recent hip surgery and her own medical problems, Grace volunteered to give me a tour of the town that had been Dr. Fuller's home for so many years. Following Solomon, Jr.'s death, his son, Dr. John Lewis Fuller, granted me access to Dr. Fuller's files and papers and has provided continued support in this project.

Acknowledgments are especially due the University of South Florida's Institute on Black Life for supporting my research on Dr. Fuller through a Faculty Research Development Grant in 2001 and to Dr. William Haley, Director of the Aging Studies Program at the University of South Florida, for allowing me to take the time necessary to complete this project.

The collection of data for this project spanned a period of ten years and included travel to Massachusetts, Virginia, West Virginia, Washington, D.C., New Hampshire, and New York, as well as to Frankfurt and Munich, Germany. In my search for information about Dr. Fuller, I found that those who had known him or who were familiar with his work had only words of praise for him and were pleased that his achievements would be recognized. I am thankful to Dr. Orlando Lightfoot, Professor of Psychiatry at the Clinical and Community Psychiatry Center at Boston University Medical Center for encouraging me to begin this project and for identifying sources of information. I also wish to thank Dr. Jean Wilkinson, former Director of The Solomon Carter Fuller Mental Health Center in Boston, Dr. Tommy Bogger, Director of H.B. Wilson Archives at Norfolk State University, Dr. Konrad Maurer, Department of Psychiatry and Psychotherapy at the Johann Wolfgang Goethe University in Frankfort and his wife, Ulrike Maurer, Dr. G. Neundorfer at the Psychiatric Institute, Ludwig-Maximilians University in Munich, Lucretia McClure at the Francis A. Countway Library of Medicine, Boston Medical Library-Harvard Medical Library, Emily Beattie, Alumni Medical Library at the Boston University School of Medicine, Dorothy Mosakowski, Coordinator of Archives at Clark University, Dr. Phyllis Galloway, Director of the Heritage Hall Archives and Research Center at Livingstone College in Salisbury, North Carolina, Susan Heffner, Director of Archives at the American Psychiatric Association, Steven Scheibel, Administrator at Westborough State Hospital, Dr. Klaus Hamann, Massachusetts General Hospital, The Framingham Historical Society, Elaine Pinderhughes, Boston, Dr. Beatrice Reynolds, Sidney, Maine, and Ruth Ballou, Keene, New Hampshire for information and access to source material.

My sincere appreciation goes to Drew Smith, University of South Florida School of Library and Information Science, for his work in formatting the manuscript.

I am grateful to my colleagues, friends, and family for their advice and support. Special thanks to my father, Dr. Alfred R. Henderson, who inspired me to begin this project and who helped to interpret Dr. Fuller's scientific research. And finally, to my husband, Roy – my love and appreciation for your faith in my ability to pull this together and your support during the ten years that it took to do so.

Introduction

Fuller's Arrival in Germany 1905

Can a people....live and develop over three hundred years simply by reacting? Are American Negroes simply the creation of white men, or have they at least helped to create themselves out of what they found around them?[1]
Ralph Ellison, *Shadow and Act*

As the slender young man stepped off the train in Munich, he was about to begin what was to become an important journey in his pursuit of knowledge that would significantly influence his medical research and practice in the years to come. A new psychiatric clinic was opening at the University of Munich under the direction of Dr. Emil Kraepelin, noted for his revolutionary ideas in the classification of mental illness and the treatment of psychiatric patients.[2] Dr. Solomon Carter Fuller had traveled to Germany to study under Kraepelin and to take courses in pathology for the purpose of improving his skills in analyzing brain tissue as it related to mental illness.

Fuller was one of the estimated 15,000 Americans who traveled to Europe between 1870 and 1914 for the purpose of advanced medical education and training. Much of the medical knowledge that American physicians would bring back to the United States was based on experimental science and would eventually lead to a change in American medical practice from that of lay people and unqualified healers to professional physicians.[3] This freedom of movement allowing students to travel from university to university and from one country to another in pursuit of an education would come to a halt in 1914 as Europe began to mobilize for an impending war.

In many instances whether or not much or anything was learned, they seemed to feel that it gave a badge of distinction and most of all, enhanced their learning capacity. Of course, I lay myself open to the same change, but I think another motive prompted, something in the nature of a challenge and while my judgment might not have been of the best, there was absolutely nothing the matter with my courage.[4]

While it was not unusual for Americans to leave the United States for a foreign land to take advantage of learning opportunities during this time, it took a great deal of courage and perseverance for Solomon Fuller, an African American, to achieve this goal. As he walked from the Munich train station to his hotel that cold winter night, Fuller could not help but think of another man who had left the United States fifty-three years earlier for a better life in Liberia – his grandfather, John Lewis Fuller, a slave who bought his freedom and whose courage inspired Solomon throughout his life.

Over forty-five years later, Solomon Fuller was encouraged by his son, Solomon, Jr., to tell the story of his life:

You can tell a story which except for a very few people has been unobserved and untold. Our country has been built by courageous pioneers who for the most part have remained individually obscure, but who nevertheless have been typified in American drama, art and literature. However, until recently overlooked and neglected, some of our pioneers are now being pictured in the light of oppression and the depravity of a minority people. I need not say this is the story of the American Negro. I believe that even though popular attention is being given him, the Negro American is losing much of the current and recent past story of his development. A very important part of this development can be told by you as you have lived it and seen it. A story of modest and quiet achievement, a story that is perhaps more commonplace than anybody would believe until it was first told. I suppose there are many who could tell it but I believe none with more genuine simplicity than you – a story of success and unadvertised life fulfillment among our people....I believe that you can see the value of such a literary work. One that needs to be told now lest it be lost in the struggle for advancement and integration in American culture....Even if you decide not to do this, undoubtedly you will want to make a contribution to the story by revealing information about yourselves and the people you have known.[5]

At first, Fuller was not receptive to his son's request to tell the story of his achievements. "My wife has been the achiever. I don't attach any importance to what I personally have done. A person who writes an autobiography, I often wonder if they are telling the truth about themselves."

Sol Jr. persisted in urging his father to tell his story. To facilitate the story-telling process, he purchased a tape recorder so that Fuller, who by this time had lost most of his sight, could dictate his memories and thoughts. His wife could then type his accounts and the tapes could be reused – a feature that appealed to

Fuller's frugal nature. He finally agreed to create a record of his life for the benefit of his family:

> Well I suppose what you say has its merits and advantages and things of that sort, but there are so many people whose lives have been far more interesting. Now I have had in mind for a long time, and Sol has more or less encouraged it, was to write a little account of how our family, the Fuller part of it anyway, and how it came about, and while I don't believe so much in ancestry worship I do think it has some value. At least ought to have some value for one's progeny.[6]

Although Solomon Carter Fuller never published the story of his life, he did manage to record some of his family history and some of his significant life events and accomplishments. These papers, which included both typed and handwritten notes, were found in the basement of his son's Cape Cod home and passed on to his grandson, John L. Fuller. Solomon Fuller titled his story "Where My Caravan Has Rested". He selected this title to represent the story of one man's journey along the road of life.

> ....a caravan suggests a company of travelers – no man goes through life alone. But is in general accompanied by fellows from the time of his birth to the end of his life. And there are many things which influence a man's life – those things which we call necessities of life – shelter, food and we might add as an essential, the reproduction of the species....We think of a caravan traveling a dusty desert of sand, with here and there an oasis – well these oases in general are the bright spots in a man's life. There is seldom a being to whom life is just one big oasis – it has its various ups and downs.[7]

Fifty years have passed since Solomon Carter Fuller's "caravan" came to the end of its journey. Like many heroes of color, African American scientists were systematically ignored by the writers of history. The story of Fuller's life provides a glimpse of a man whose achievements in medicine and science were many, despite the racial oppression that existed in the United States in the early 20th century. Here was a man who made important contributions to Alzheimer's disease research and to the development of American psychiatry. Yet few people know anything about Solomon Fuller today.

The material for Dr. Fuller's biography has been collected from his personal notes and interviews with family members and members of the medical and scientific communities who are familiar with his work. In addition, the author has traveled to the University of Munich in Germany – the site of Fuller's introduction to the neuropathology of dementia, and has spent many hours in archives on slavery and the colonization of Liberia. In the search for records of Fuller's family members who lived in Virginia during the time of slavery, it soon became apparent that they had lived in a period of our country's history when being black meant being invisible and where the written account of the world of the average black citizen was generally silent. The traditional sources of historical information such as records, manuscripts and documents are seldom available prior to the turn of the century for black people. Only small fragments of their individual histories survive. It was also difficult to obtain additional information about Fuller's life in Liberia. The recent conflict in that area of Africa has led to destruction of government buildings and records, and has resulted in the disruption of mail service.

Fuller's life story and the sweeping changes that occurred in the past two centuries are intertwined. This connection between the personal and the historical provides a window onto this era of change.

Chapter One

The Beginning: John Lewis Fuller
Norfolk, Virginia
1830

...every time a black man sets down to write a coming-of-age memoir he
must drag after him hundreds of years of history. Race is still the subject.[1]
Judith Dunford, *New York Times Book Review*

I have only the faintest memory of John Lewis Fuller, who died when I
was between four and five. In many ways, this John Lewis Fuller was quite a
remarkable man. He was not noted for any great learning, but he certainly was
a most practical sort of fellow, and from difficult surroundings he grasped a
very desirable economic place in the times and circumstances in which he
lived. None of his descendents have been great people, as the World measures
greatness, but I think most of them have been good citizens of their
communities, and have contributed to civic life to the extent of their abilities.[2]

They lived in back alleys, cellars, factory lofts and abandoned industrial
sites located near the docks off Water Street. Referred to as free Negroes, they
had come to Norfolk, Virginia with hopes and dreams of starting a new life and
putting behind them the memories and scars of slavery.

Born in 1794, John Lewis Fuller had spent most of his life in slavery,
working as a skilled boot and shoemaker for his white master in nearby
Petersburg. Many slave owners encouraged their slaves to become craftsmen
for both the work that they could do on their plantation, as well as for the wages
they would bring when hired out to other plantations. To John Fuller,

apprenticeship to a master tradesman was a step towards independence, since his master allowed him to save a portion of his earnings to buy his freedom. Under a law passed in 1782, Virginia permitted slave owners to free their slaves.[3] Freedom was achieved through miscegenation (interbreeding), the death of a master as stipulated in his will, meritorious service, or as in Fuller's case, accumulating enough capital to buy one's freedom.

John also saved enough money to buy the freedom of a white indentured servant he had fallen in love with, known only as Nancy. Nancy was one of a large number of settlers at that time who had come to America from England under contract to serve for a specified number of years or until they were twenty-one, as repayment for their ocean passage.[4] Friendships between black slaves and white indentured servants developed as the two groups worked side by side. A common bond was created by the sharing of a hard life and exploitation. John had not allowed himself to develop relationships with Negro women because he was determined that no child of his would be born a slave. The question of whether John and Nancy were legally married remains unanswered. At that time, it was illegal for a white person to intermarry with a Negro, and marriages were not documented by ministers at the black churches.

Petersburg, located south of Richmond below the falls of the Appomattox River, had a large population of free Negroes. But John and Nancy, along with many other former slaves, decided to move to the nearby port city of Norfolk which offered greater opportunities for jobs. By 1830, there were over two hundred free Negro households in Norfolk. The ambition of John Fuller was that of other Negroes in Norfolk at that time – to buy a house; pursue a trade or business; and provide for his wife and children. He refused to consider the planting of cotton or tobacco, because too many Negroes had suffered from those crops. Instead, he continued his shoe making business, teaching his sons the trade. His wife, Nancy, ran a stall in the town's public market. Their combined income was enough to provide for their growing family. "...He apparently was not an educated man, but he certainly was not an ignorant fellow. He had sufficient ability to supply the needs of his family and a little something besides."[5]

Their oldest daughter, Nancy, later referred to by Solomon Fuller as the "family shrew," returned to live in Petersburg in 1838 following her marriage to Alexander Jarratt. Alexander was a member of a prominent free Negro family, whose members were part Indian and were said to have been descendents of the famed Pocahontas Tribe. The Jarratts lived on an island across from Petersburg, known as Pocahontas Village and owned a profitable boating business.[6] Alexander's travels as a boat steward in his family's business often took him to Norfolk which enabled him to maintain contact with his wife's family. In a letter written to his wife during one of his trips to Norfolk in 1838, he assured her that her mother, brothers and sisters were pleased with the presents that she had sent them.

...Your mother, father, sisters and brothers are well. Sister Becky says that she is very much pleased with her baget and thanks you ontel [sic] you are better paid. She expects to leave when her month is up to assist your mother in the market.

Mother was pleased with your present and says that they are very nice. They wants to see you very much indeed and says they shall expect you on my return trip. I could say a great deal more but time will not admit therefore I must conclude with remaining your sincere and loving husband ontel [sic] Death do part."[7]

In addition to Nancy, the Fullers had seven other children: John Lewis, Jr., Rebecca, Henry, Sarah, Thomas, Margaret, and Solomon, the father of Solomon Carter Fuller. Two of the children, John Lewis, Jr. and Margaret, died in early childhood.

While his white wife and eight mulatto children caused John Fuller to have some attachment to the white race, there were also powerful forces in American society that made for hatred of whites and that gave him strong ties to blacks.

No colored man was really free while residing in a slave state. He was ever more or less subject to the condition of his slave brother. In his color was his badge of bondage.[8]

By 1830, the number of free Negroes had grown considerably.[9] It was felt that the presence of free Negroes set a bad example for slaves, and lawmakers were convinced that they had to limit the size of this increasing population and to place additional restrictions on them in order to maintain their slave society. A campaign of defamation was carried out to keep them in their place. Following the Nat Turner slave rebellion of 1831, laws were passed that restricted the freedom of free Negroes to participate in political, social, religious, and economic activities.[10] Many states established laws that prohibited them from assembling without white supervision and preventing them from holding certain jobs. Most southern states prohibited black preachers from conducting religious services, insisting that white clergy be present at all church gatherings. In Norfolk, curfews were imposed on free Negroes, requiring them to be home by ten o'clock at night or risk being imprisoned and fined. City ordinances forbid them to own firearms or dogs. Free Negroes also had higher mortality rates than slaves, due to the fact that slaves had masters who would arrange for their medical care. Tuberculosis and cholera were the main causes of death for free Negroes. Norfolk's cholera epidemic in 1832 claimed many black victims due to their poor sanitation and living conditions. Even in death was the condition of the free Negro apparent.

One day a funeral passed my grandfather's shop, there were just a few people following and the coffin was so poorly constructed with great big cracks that you could see the body through the coffin. That so enraged him that a man should be buried in that fashion."[11]

As the status of the free Negro continued to deteriorate, John Fuller began to give serious consideration to his safety and that of his family. Fearing the spread of slave rebellion, whites were directing their actions of persecution toward free Negroes. Assaults were common as whites demanded the removal of free Negroes from their communities. A gathering of family or friends was always in danger of being broken up by police or white vigilantes. "Cases have been known where freemen, being called upon by a pack of ruffians to show their free papers, have presented them, when the ruffians have torn them up, seized the victim and sold him to a life of endless bondage."[12]

Adding to this constant state of fear was John Fuller's growing frustration at his ability to educate and financially support his family.[13] Although most blacks were not allowed to attend schools, a school for free Negroes had been established in Norfolk and many blacks were taught to read and write in the basements of white churches. Following the Nat Turner Rebellion, most Southern states passed laws that made it illegal to educate blacks, closing the schools that had been established by free Negroes. In 1837, the Virginia Legislature passed a law that barred black children who had been educated outside of the state from returning to Virginia. The depressed economy in Norfolk had restricted the prosperity of free Negroes. The influx of immigrants from Ireland and Germany increased competition between white and black workers, with white men replacing free Negroes in most of the skilled trades.

The poor economic and social conditions of free Negroes in the United States led many blacks to consider leaving the country. The idea of sending blacks to another country was not new, but one that had been supported by some Americans with dubious motives. Many white Americans were concerned that the black population was increasing faster than the white population and southern slave owners worried about the influence of free Negroes on slave insurrections.[14]

> Of all the classes of our population, the most vicious is that of the free colored. It is the inevitable result of their moral, political and evil degradation. Contaminated themselves, they extended their vices all around them, to the slaves, to the whites.
> Henry Clay, *Tenth Annual Report of the American Colonization Society*, 1826.

The American Society for Colonizing Free People of Color in the United States had been created in 1816 to establish a Negro colony in Africa with the aid of federal and state governments and to influence public opinion to support the project. The organization, its name later changed to the American Colonization Society, was commissioned to find a suitable location for colonization on the west African coast and to facilitate the transportation of those free Negroes who wished to resettle. Following the passage of the 1819 law that prohibited slave trade in the United States, the Colonization Society was also given the responsibility of resettling blacks who were taken from slave traders' ships.

In 1822 land was purchased and by 1824 the settlement of Liberia (land of freedom) had been established with Monrovia, named in honor of President Monroe, as its capital. Norfolk was one of the first cities in Virginia to have a chapter of the American Colonization Society. Many free Negroes distrusted the organization, perceiving colonization as being a way to make the institution of slavery more secure by removing them from the country. But as social and economic conditions for free Negroes deteriorated, Liberia was increasingly seen as a refuge from persecution and an opportunity for a better life.

> Now, I don't know just where John Lewis stood on that idea, but certainly it was that he had formerly been in favor among those who believed that the Constitution should mean what it says. However this group sort of lost hope after the Nat Turner insurrection in Virginia. So he decided to take his chances with those who maintained colonial views.[15]

By 1847, John's wife, Nancy had died. His daughter, Sarah kept house for her father. Solomon, Solomon Carter's father, and at age 12, John's youngest child, was sent to live with his married sister, Rebecca Nimmo. It is not known for certain if John remarried, but there is a record of marriage between a John Fuller and Nancy Brown, free persons of color on May 25, 1848.[16] In 1849, John Fuller sent his son, Thomas to Liberia with friends. Tom was known for his high spirit and short temper, and his father was afraid that he would get into trouble with the whites in the area.

At first, John Fuller rejected the idea of leaving the United States. His progressive discontent with lack of political and social freedom for free Negroes and the increasing restrictions placed on his life and the lives of his family during the years following the Nat Turner insurrection eventually caused him to reconsider the idea. Solomon would later explain that his grandfather's decision to go to Liberia was made because

> It was so dangerous for free col. people (picked up as runaway slaves). ....Grandfather was convinced that, despite the racist motives of some of the supporters of the American Colonization Society, life would be better in Liberia than in white America. Grandfather took family back to Monrovia for safety – hated U.S.[17]

Chapter Two

A New Life in Africa
Monrovia
1852

John Lewis Fuller and his family were among the estimated 18,000 black immigrants that were brought to the coast of West Africa by the American Colonization Society (ACS) between 1820 and 1867. The first group of settlers had established a colony on Sherbrook, a small island near Sierra Leone. The area's harsh climate, tropical diseases, and hostile natives made life difficult for the settlers. After many of them died from malaria, those who survived voted to give up the idea of settling in Africa and prepared to return to the United States. A settler by the name of Elijah Johnson saved the day. He rose and declared that he and his family came from the United States to the promised land and that the rest of the settlers could go if they wanted to, but he and his family expected to live in Africa until they died.[1] His firm stand inspired the others to change their minds, and the small group then moved to a site further down the coast.

Two years later, accompanied by another shipload of immigrants from the United States, the colonists arrived on the shores of West Africa in an area known as the forest belt. An American Negro trader, Joseph Roberts, who had settled in the area, joined forces with the colonists. Roberts and the agent appointed by the ACS, a white man named Jehudi Ashmun, led the colony for several years.[2] The name Liberia, taken from the word liberty, was adopted by the colonists, and its capital, Monrovia, was named for President James Monroe.

The first years down there in Monrovia, [*sic*] the first years in Plymouth, Mass. was not a bit worse to the immigrants to Plymouth settlement than the suffering in Liberia. [Jehudi Ashmun] worked just as hard as any of them in the establishment of the town of Monrovia and when I was a boy, the principle street was Ashmand Street. We lived on Ashmand Street and it was named for Yehudi Ashmand.[3]

In 1824, Liberia's first constitution was ratified, which defined the immigrants' rights and responsibilities and granted the ACS governor the power to enforce the laws. Support for the ACS weakened in 1832 when the settlement was unable to absorb the 1,066 immigrants who arrived as a result of the new restrictions that were imposed upon free Negroes by southern states. Two hundred sixty-two of the new immigrants died within one year of their arrival. The outrage that followed soon caused a split in the organization, resulting in the formation of independent colonization societies that founded separate West African colonies. Most of these colonies were eventually consolidated into the Commonwealth of Liberia, established in 1839. Over the next seven years, an internal political struggle began to emerge between the settlers, now calling themselves Americo-Liberians, and the ACS. The ACS agreed to relinquish its authority over the colony, and in 1847, Liberia became the first republic in Africa, electing Joseph Jenkins Roberts, a free Negro from Virginia as its first president.[4]

On November 27, 1852, John Fuller, accompanied by his youngest son, Solomon, his daughter, Rebecca, her husband and three children, sailed from Baltimore for Liberia, a trip lasting approximately forty days. His first glimpse of what was to be his new home was an area located eight miles north of Monrovia near the junction of the St. Paul River and Stockton Creek. For the next six months, this was to be their residence, as was the custom for all new immigrants. The long low brick building that housed the new arrivals was divided into small rooms that opened into a common hall. In each room was a bed, a table and a few chairs.[5] In addition to providing housing and food for the Fuller family's first six months in Liberia, the ACS also paid for their passage on the ship, which amounted to sixty dollars a person.

When John Lewis Fuller and his family left the immigrants' residence in the summer of 1852 and arrived in Monrovia, they found a small, unimpressive cluster of buildings situated on streets that were overgrown with bramble bush, leaving only a narrow path for pedestrians. There were several government buildings. One, a wooden structure, served as the headquarters of the president, secretaries, and post master, and contained a small printing office. Two stone buildings housed the courts, the senate chamber, and the House of Representatives and nearby, stood a rickety old jail. Other public buildings included Methodist, Baptist and Presbyterian churches, an academy and a high school. There were seven brick houses and a few frame houses, but most colonists lived in dilapidated frame and bamboo huts. Due to the difficulty in clearing the dense brush, there was little agriculture and few livestock, with the exception of family-owned cows, sheep, goats, hogs, and turkeys. The introduction of domestic animals proved to be challenging because of widespread disease. Settlers were introduced to the native African diet, its staples of rice and cassada – a coarse, tough, tasteless root, and the exotic fruits of the land – plantains, oranges, lemons, tamarind, and cocoa nut.

For John Lewis Fuller, the small settlement of Liberia represented the promise of freedom from the racism of America, and he was determined not to let the hardships of his new home discourage him. Situated on Cape Montserrado, the land was a swamp, overgrown with mangrove and dragon's blood bushes. The tide would rise over much of the area's river banks twice a day, leaving a foul odor. The rivers contained crocodiles and hippopotamuses, and numerous elephants, leopards, tigers, and monkeys roamed the dense forests. Additional hazards were the plentiful reptiles and insects such as boa constrictors, cobras, termites, and flesh-eating ants. The harsh climate added to the settlers' distress, with temperatures that averaged ninety-six degrees in the shade. Seasons were divided into wet and dry. Beginning in May and ending in November, the wet season brought constant, torrential rains and occasional tornados. During the dry season, there was seldom any rain. Disease was rampant and mortality high. All colonists experienced the "fever" upon arrival and many contracted other diseases such as the cran-cran, which affects the skin; the jiggers, which is caused by an insect that incubates and forms ulcers; and the sleeping disease, that usually resulted in death.

Most settlers who survived their first year in Liberia achieved a reasonable standard of living. A select few found success and a sense of freedom that was not possible during that time for their black families and friends in America. The fact that there was very little European trade and interest in the area was an advantage for the immigrants who had the freedom to establish their settlements with little interference from other countries. Many settlers were employed by the Missionary and Colonization Societies, trading rum, tobacco, cotton cloth and trinkets to the natives for palm oil and camwood, which were then traded again to merchant ships. Most of those who succeeded were skilled artisans and craftsmen.

> [John Fuller] continued his shoe making business when he left for Liberia and all of his boys were taught that trade. He took an active part in the civic life in Liberia, and founded what was probably the first charitable organization in Liberia – the Mechanics Charitable Society of Monrovia – which still exists, which has some of the fine characteristics of the Charitable Mechanics Society here in Boston.[6]

Responding to the increasing need for skilled laborers in the building of the settlement, John Fuller became a carpenter and a brickmaker. His brick making business prospered, as did his later efforts at tobacco farming.

The Fullers soon became one of the leading families in Liberia. Solomon Carter Fuller would later attribute his family's contribution to the development of the small republic to his grandfather's attitude and example, which promoted the family ethos that emphasis should be placed on service. John's son, Thomas, who had been sent to Liberia by his family three years prior to their arrival because of his militant behavior, had directed his energy into the development of Monrovia. Tom became a probate judge and later served two terms as Mayor of Monrovia. As a Senator for the Liberian state of Maryland in 1857, Tom signed an agreement of annexation making Maryland a county in the Republic.[7]   John's oldest son, Henry, was the last of his children to come to Liberia, arriving in 1856. Henry had enlisted in the Navy in 1852 as a landsman and sailed on the USS Powhatan. While stationed in Japan, he served as a mess steward for Commodore Perry. Arriving back in Norfolk after his discharge from the Navy in 1856, Henry found that his family had immigrated to Liberia. He soon followed them, taking the first available ship. Upon his arrival, he joined his father in the building of the settlement, working as a contractor and builder. Before long, Henry left his father's business and set out to build churches in outlying districts, later becoming a Methodist minister. Solomon Fuller, John's third son and the father of Solomon Carter Fuller, became a successful coffee planter and for many years, was the high sheriff of Montserrado County, Liberia.

Solomon Carter Fuller was born on August 11, 1872 in his family's house on Ashmand Street in Monrovia. His mother, Anna Ursala James, was the daughter of medical missionaries, Benjamin Van Rensalaer James and Margaret Stewart. A descendant of two prominent New York families, Van Ransalaer and James, and also reported to be related to Sally Hemings, Benjamin Van Rensalaer James was a free mulatto who had come to Liberia in 1829 to serve as a Presbyterian medical missionary. There, he joined other missionaries who came from North America and Europe to spread Christianity. As part of their humanitarian mission, they set up hospitals and medical clinics. Although he lacked a formal degree in medicine, B. V. R. James had obtained his medical knowledge by attending lectures in the United States and in Edinburgh, Scotland.

> Now we went to see Pr. Pierce, formerly Rector of St. Andrews in Framingham, one Sunday at Newport some years ago – and he took me around and we went to the Newport Yacht Club and on the wall of the yacht club was a portrait of Commodore James – former commodore of the New York Yacht Club and he was the spitting image of my Grandpa B. V. R. James. He could easily have passed, looking at the two portraits....you could say either could be Commodore James.[8]

Shortly after B. V. R. James' arrival in Liberia, he married Margaret Stewart, a free mulatto who had left her home in Charleston, South Carolina to teach the children of Liberian colonists. Margaret soon joined her husband in his medical missionary work and when he died, she took up his satchel and continued practicing medicine. Rev. James died before Solomon Carter Fuller was born, but his memories of his grandmother, Margaret, influenced his early interest in medicine. "She had the use of only one hand due to an infection, but could do more with one hand than most women can do with two."

Anna Ursula James was born in Half Cavalla, Maryland County, Liberia, one of seven children and the only daughter of B. V. R. and Margaret Stewart James. A widow, she married Solomon Fuller in 1871. Anna's teaching experience led her to organize a school on their coffee plantation for her two sons, Solomon Carter and his younger brother, Thomas George. Soon, the school's enrollment grew to include children from nearby plantations.

It wasn't long before Liberia's boundaries were extended through trade and agreements made between the colonists and the native tribes. Land was obtained from local chiefs by giving them gifts and money and sometimes by force. Many of the tribes resented the colonists and frequent skirmishes took place, particularly in that part of Liberia known as Maryland.[9]

> They were always fighting Grebos (a native African tribe) out there. And the Grebos were encouraged by the European traders. You see along that area is a great African slave belt where they collect these slaves to be sent to the West Indies and America.[10]

Solomon Fuller served on the Boundary Commission of Liberia, where he worked toward the settlement of land claims between Sierra Leone and Liberia. His political position gave him significant power and control and he was frequently paid in land. By the early 1880's, the Fuller family had acquired several plots of land in the interior of the country. Some seventy years later during a conversation with his son, Solomon Carter Fuller recalled that the family had owned land in Liberia, but did not know its location or if it had been sold by his brother, Tom.

> The boundaries were pretty well settled but Sierra Leone was a much more progressive settlement and they were constantly encroaching. Now we were being encroached upon from the northwest by the British and from the Southeast by the French. Both of them took fairly good slices. They sent their traders up in there and they established themselves and they claimed that it was British Territory and the French did the same thing. In all probability (our property) is on some of the land leased by Firestone......(Tom) could have disposed of it because he had my power of attorney to dispose of any lands or realty that we might own jointly. We owned it jointly because my father died without leaving a will and we were his only heirs.[11]

Solomon Carter Fuller's family were members of the privileged class in the emerging social stratification in Liberia. The upper echelon of this class system was dominated by the Americo-Liberians, particularly those who were light skinned.[12] Next came the civilized natives, who were brought up in the homes of the ruling class, followed by the recaptured Africans who had been brought to Liberia by the United States Navy, known as the Congoes. At the bottom of the stratum were the Aborigines, the original inhabitants of the country. Americo-Liberians considered themselves superior to native Africans and scorned their culture and customs. Many pursued jobs as government officials, which were considered easy positions that offered good benefits and had few responsibilities. The Liberian Constitution prevented the native Africans from automatically becoming Liberian citizens. In order to gain voting rights or be elected to public office, they had to prove that they had owned land for at least three years, had accepted the Christian religion, and had given up their tribal customs.[13]

In an effort to eliminate the slave trade in Africa, the settlers mounted campaigns against slavery posts that continued to operate along the Liberian coast. They were not supported by all native Africans in their attempt to abolish the slave trade, as it was a main source of revenue for the coast of Africa. Despite the lack of support by some Africans, the slave trade was eliminated by the late 1850s. Although the Liberian Constitution forbade slavery, it was estimated that wealthy settlers had from ten to fifteen African servants.[14] The social culture of paternalism in Liberia was similar to the paternalism practiced by many of the members of the American Colonization Society in the United States in their relationship with their slaves. Native children were often sent to live with Americo-Liberian families by their families, who believed that the experience would enhance their social status. While some of these children were treated as servants, others were raised as members of the family. When Solomon Carter Fuller was growing up in Liberia, he had a house servant who took care of his personal needs. Years later, when questioned by his son Sol as to whether this man was a slave, Fuller insisted that although the man was not paid for his services (he was given room and board), he was not a slave.

Fuller remembered his early years in Liberia as being happy ones, living among the more influential people in his small society.

> His father had a reputation as a fine marksman. He would often take Solomon and his brother out in a carved wooden log, paddling down the river and singing along the way. The customary chant, sung in unison, would be "somboli" followed by the family name. When they would encounter another boat, a race would ensue and as one boat would pass another, it was the custom to splash. During one of these races between the Fuller's boat and a boat containing a family by the name of Roberts, the Fuller children were splashed and, as a result, became soaking wet. There was a great deal of concern about illness and disease at that time, so Solomon's father became upset and took up his gun and pointed it at the Roberts' boat. Of course he wasn't going to shoot, but those on the other boat became frightened and jumped overboard. This incident became a family joke.[15]

Solomon started school when he was five years old. Three years later, his family left Monrovia to go to Caldwell, a small settlement about twelve miles up the river. Solomon's schooling was continued by his mother, who not only instructed her sons in the basic learning skills, but also taught them Latin. By age ten, he was reading Julius Caesar in Latin. Solomon's love for the ancient language would continue throughout his life until his death, when he said his good-byes in Latin to a special friend.

Solomon was educated at home until the age of ten, when he was enrolled at a small private school about a mile from his home that was run by a West Indian Episcopalian missionary minister by the name of Gibson. While his experience at the school was a positive one, it also contributed to Solomon's later feelings of embitterment toward the church. While attending the school, he went to church services regularly. He was fascinated by the stories about the United States that told of the opportunities for education and growth, and the freedoms that were reported to exist. When he later arrived in the United States and witnessed as well as experienced discrimination and racism in American society and even in church practices, he severed his connection with the church except for relationships he had with clergy in social and professional situations.

At age twelve, he left home to attend the College Preparatory School in Monrovia, which was headed by Thomas Haines, a graduate of Liberia College. While attending the school, Solomon stayed at the home of his Aunt Rebecca Nimo and her daughter, Frances Hilton. He continued his studies in Latin and would later recall that when punished for misbehavior by an instructor or the headmaster, he would be sent to his room and assigned an extra Latin reading. Solomon was elated for it allowed him the opportunity to engage in something he enjoyed. He quickly distinguished himself academically and at age sixteen, was admitted to the sub-freshman class of Liberia College.

In March, 1889, midway through his freshman year at Liberia College, Solomon's father died. At the time of his death at age 55, the elder Solomon Fuller was the owner of one of Liberia's large coffee plantations, located along the St. Paul's River and known for its' Liberica coffees, which were sold to the United States and Europe. Although coffee had been a profitable export in the 1870s and early 1880s, increasing competition from Brazil and the West Indies had lowered the price of Liberian coffee and decreased the volume of coffee exported.[16]

The reduction in its major export was only one of several factors contributing to Liberia's severe economic decline in 1889. Poor government management, high interest from loans, and low revenues from taxes increased the financial burden faced by the country's leaders. Agriculture had remained largely undeveloped, in part because of the difficulty in cultivating the land, but also as a result of the reluctance of many of the country's settlers to engage in manual labor.

> I have seen Liberians who went to the west coast with reputations for industry sitting idly in dilapidated or rudely constructed houses, walking around abusing the government for not opening roads and building bridges, thus creating prosperity....then some have plainly said, "I worked hard enough when I was a slave. Here I can lie down when I want and get up when I please; and there is no one to molest me or make me afraid."[17]

Coming from a country where they had no civil rights and little education, most of Liberia's immigrants had not had the experience of taking control of their lives, and thus were unprepared to manage the complexities of the development of a social and political system.

The small number of schools that existed in Liberia were run by foreign missionaries and focused on religious education and preparation for government service. In 1874, the missionaries had lost the support of the government after a revolt by the Grebo Africans who had been educated and supported by the Episcopalian Mission School. Following the revolt, missionary activities were restricted by the government, thus preventing the establishment of new schools for the Africans. By the late 1800s, a government education system had been established and in 1863, Liberia College opened its doors to students. From the start, the college experienced problems with faculty supervision of its students and the poor conditions of its campus buildings.[18]

The deteriorating conditions in his country and the poor quality of its education system were concerns to young Solomon as he thought about his future and his dream of becoming a physician. In June, 1889, three months after his father's death, Solomon Carter Fuller left Liberia for the United States to pursue his dream.

Chapter Three

In Pursuit of a Dream
North Carolina
1889

Thirty-seven years had passed since John Lewis Fuller had left the United States for a better life in Liberia. There had been many changes affecting black Americans that had taken place since Solomon's grandfather's departure in 1851. The Reconstruction period following the Civil War saw the addition of the Thirteenth, Fourteenth, and Fifteenth Amendments to the U.S. Constitution, which had resulted in the abolition of slavery, granted civil rights to black Americans, and guaranteed black men the right to vote.[1] Despite the legal protection promised, blacks in the southern states were denied these new rights by state legislatures, federal courts or congressional action. By the time that Solomon set foot on American soil, laws that enforced racial segregation, especially in the south, were in effect. Public facilities such as toilets, water fountains, parks, beaches, hospitals, and schools were segregated, as well as public transportation. The lynching of blacks carried out by vigilantes seeking revenge for an actual or fabricated crime had become a means of keeping them "in their place" and had risen to epidemic proportions in the south.

In September, 1889, Solomon Carter Fuller arrived at Livingstone College in Salisbury, North Carolina, a school founded in 1879 for black students and affiliated with the African Methodist Episcopal Church. The only member of his family to return to the United States, he came to stay just until he became qualified to practice medicine. He then planned to return to Liberia to continue his grandparents' medical missionary work. One of the first students from

Africa to attend Livingstone College, Solomon was barely seventeen when he arrived in the United States.

> It so happens that the train which brought me to Salisbury arrived late at night. Dr. Price (the President of Livingstone College) was also a passenger, but it was not until after we left the train, I noticed he was observing me. He came to where I was standing and asked if I were the boy from Liberia.....He took me to his home where I remained for two days. The next day being Sunday the household assembled for family prayer before breakfast. Each person in attendance read a verse from the selected chapter of the Bible and when it came my turn, out of the corner of my eye I could see him watching me intently and then relaxing after I had gone about halfway through the verse.[2]

For the next four years, Fuller lived with his classmates in a crowded, three-story residence hall on the small campus. At Livingstone, like other religiously sponsored colleges, students were expected to uphold strict moral codes. Smoking and drinking were forbidden and there were few opportunities for students to venture off the campus, which was situated in rural western North Carolina.

Fuller's class of 1893 was the last class to graduate under the presidency of Dr. Joseph Charles Price, who died a few months after his graduation. Fifty years later, when Solomon was invited to accept an honorary degree at Livingstone, he paid tribute to Dr. Price and his influence on the quality of liberal arts education for students at a time when the focus was on vocational education for black youth in the South. Booker T. Washington thought like most of the whites during that time, that a liberal arts curriculum was not feasible for black students, but that they should instead learn manual skills

> Mr. Booker T. Washington, one of the most noted of Southerners of his time had made his famous Atlanta speech while I was a senior here. This speech did much to influence the educational program for American Negroes, with result that the schools for a so-called liberal which had done much for Am. education and progress in general, suffered greatly where Negroes were concerned. The stress was placed on economics. Dr. Price had no objection to economic advances, in fact welcomed it – Heart, Head and Hand I had often heard in these halls. Now this you need not be told for you have known as well as anyone. The fact however remains, Livingstone and colleges like Livingstone where the liberal arts were stressed, suffered greatly. Our greater leader gone to his reward, others have carried on, doggedly, with great faith, high aspirations, toiling ceaselessly, often without reward but always with confidence.[3]

By 1890, most of the southern states had repealed the civil rights laws passed during the reconstruction period. As a result, a new system of racial segregation and discrimination emerged, referred to as "Jim Crow". Unlike blacks who grew up in the south in the late 1800s and faced daily humiliation and threats in a segregated society, Fuller had enjoyed a childhood of privilege and was not prepared for the racism that he encountered and would later relate to his family and friends. His family status in Liberia had provided opportunities for him to attend the country's best schools and he did not have the feeling of being inferior. Despite the racist environment that he found himself in, the high priority placed on education by the Fuller family and Solomon's own expectations and determination prevailed. For four years he stood at the head of his class, graduating with Honors in May, 1893.

> Mr. Fuller was not an orator, he did not have the voice; but he was a pleasing speaker and there was a sweetness in his voice which held you. But a fair writer, his strength lay in his scholarship. His was a vigorous intellect.[4]

Solomon received $150 from his mother to pay for his education at Livingstone and paid for the rest of his expenses by working in the printing office of the Livingstone College Press as a typesetter. His responsibilities at the printing office included working on the *Star of Zion*, the weekly paper for the A.M.E. Zion Church.

When classes let out for the summer, Fuller would travel north to stay at the New York City home of his cousins, the Jarratts. Riding the train to New York was a degrading experience – Fuller was forced to ride in the "colored" car, which was usually located behind the engine and was often dirty and poorly maintained. Since he could not get served in the train's lunch room, he frequently went without food or drink. In New York, Fuller would seek summer jobs in nearby hotels to earn money to pay for his college expenses. Starting out at as bellhop at the Murray Hill Hotel in New York, he later worked as a waiter at several of the large resort hotels in the Catskill Mountains in New York and in Long Branch, New Jersey.

While achieving academic success, Fuller also found time to participate in many activities on campus. In addition to tutoring other students, he managed the football team and became the president of his fraternity. When he was not involved in school activities, Fuller would relax by playing his guitar. His lack of musical talent was noted by a columnist in the school's newspaper, "I heard Sol Fuller play the guitar the other night while Harry Wood sang 'Jesus Locked the Lion's Jaw.' I never want to hear it again. Sol! Why persecuteth me?"[5]

By the time Fuller graduated from Livingstone in 1893, his contributions to the college were numerous. He had written the first class ode, was one of the authors of the college yell, and had participated in the writing of the college song. He also chose the college colors, which were later adopted by the school. In 1943, fifty years after his graduation, Livingstone College presented Fuller with an honorary degree of Doctor of Science and proclaimed him one of the school's outstanding graduates.

At a time when most medical schools refused to admit Negro students, Fuller was admitted to the Long Island College Hospital's medical degree program.[6] In March, 1894, Fuller traveled north to Brooklyn, New York, to begin his medical training. Feeling that he should no longer be financially dependent on his family, he refused all offers of assistance and earned his tuition by working as a waiter in a boarding house. Shortly after he began his studies in New York, Fuller learned of the Hayden Scholarship, established by a black man to provide financial assistance to black students at Harvard. Arriving in Cambridge, he found that the fund was not yet available. Thinking that this would be his only chance to see Boston, he decided to make the most of the opportunity. As he strolled through the city, he found himself at Boston University, where he made his way to the administrative offices and introduced himself to the dean.

In the fall of that year, Fuller transferred to Boston University School of Medicine. It was reported that he was offered financial assistance on the condition that he would agree to return to Africa as a medical missionary.[7] Fuller refused to accept funding under those conditions and entered the program without financial aid. The university accepted his personal note for his tuition. He earned this and his living expenses working as an elevator operator in a large apartment house on Commonwealth Avenue for four dollars a week. After a full day of classes, he would report for work at 6:00 in the evening and work until midnight. On Sundays, he would work from noon to midnight. He studied when not busy at work, usually between the hours of 8:30 pm and 11:00 pm. Fuller's schedule left him little time to explore Boston.

> One summer while I was in medical school I worked at the Manhattan Beach Hotel where Sousa, then a young man was giving his brilliant concerts every day in the forenoon and the afternoon. My first and only view of a regular horse race was one afternoon I went to see the races at Sheepshead Bay. Of course I didn't bet anything on them because money was too precious to throw away on horses but I wanted to see them run and then later I was at a sulky race – near Boston in a racing park.[8]

Unlike the rural, predominately white and racially restrictive environment of the South, which had been Fuller's home for the past four years, Boston was a bustling city of approximately a half-million inhabitants, representing at least twenty-five nationalities.[9] Although he had little time to enjoy the city's attractions, Fuller was impressed by the variety of its cultural life and opportunities for scientific and medical studies.

Inspired by Dr. Elmer Southard, the Director of the Boston Psychopathic Hospital and a member of the Boston University Medical School faculty, Fuller became interested in the study of neuropathology, a relative newcomer to the basic medical sciences. Remembered by Fuller as "a great teacher, a great histologist", Southard was instrumental in establishing for the first time in the history of psychiatry, the cause of a mental disease (syphilitic psychoses) as well as a specific drug to treat the disease.[10]

Fuller maintained his grueling schedule until the middle of his senior year in medical school. He then received a small grant from the Board of Donations for Education in Liberia, which enabled him to spend more time to prepare for his final examinations. Although Fuller accepted the funds from Liberia with the understanding that he would return to the country upon graduation to practice medicine, he was beginning to reconsider his plans for the future. While his commitment to return to Liberia and to his family was still strong, Fuller's growing interest in the specialization of neuropathology would soon force him to make a decision that would change the course of his life.

Chapter Four

Learning and Teaching
Boston
1897

All 'first blacks" become conditioned to racism and do not allow it
to intrude upon their missions or goals. To become a 'first black' one
had to force himself to accept bias as a way of life, to wink at it, blink
at it, and become blind if necessary to its dehumanizing methodology.
Charles H. King, Jr., *Fire in My Bones*[1]

While a medical student at Boston University, Solomon Fuller had attracted the
attention of Dr. Edward P. Colby, a professor of neurology who was impressed
by his understanding and proficiency in this specialty. Following his graduation
in 1897, Dr. Colby arranged for Fuller to meet with Dr. George Adams, the
superintendent of Westboro Insane Hospital. The hospital, on the former site of
the State Reform School for Boys, located 35 miles west of Boston, had been
established in 1884 to provide homeopathic treatment for the mentally ill in
Massachusetts, and was now in the process of creating a pathology laboratory.[2]
At a time when only 50 percent of physicians went into hospital internships and
there were deliberate policies of discrimination against Jews, women, and blacks
in most hospitals, the chance to work at Westboro offered an exceptional
opportunity for the new graduate.

For three weeks following graduation I had nothing to do and was in
rather strained financial circumstances. And one day there came to me one of
my old classmates whose father had been a professor at the Med. School, BU

with a message that his father would like to see me at his office that afternoon. When I got there, there was Dr. Adams the Supt. of the Westboro St. Hosp. Apparently the old Prof. Colby had been trying to get something for me to do in a hospital.   And Dr Adams agreed he would take me there and he asked whether I wanted to go as an interne [*sic*] for 3 or 6 months without pay or to be an interne [*sic*] and help in the Pathological Lab at Westboro which at that time was being conducted by Dr. Edward Mellis.   That position paid $20 a month board and lodging and my laundry.[3]

The decision was not easy as both offers provided opportunities for advancement in the hospital. The first offer held the possibility of progressing to a permanent staff position upon the successful completion of a short internship. This appealed to Fuller, who realized that that he had the intellectual competence to gain a position on the basis of his merits.

It would have been to the ordinary person that in a course of time after he had shown that he had aptitude for taking care of mental patients and learned something about it he would have gotten a permanent position on the staff and work his way up even to a superintendency.[4]

But Fuller realized that he was not "ordinary" and because of his color, could not hope for advancement on the basis of competence. His decision to accept the second offer was also influenced by the challenge of working in a new and developing field where he could apply his practice of reading, reflecting, searching and associating in a scholarly way. Convinced that medical progress depended on experimentation and observation, Fuller chose to go into the laboratory and use his microscope in what would be the beginning of a lifelong fascination with the structure and complexities of the brain.

The opportunity was to investigate the scientific side of mental disorders. And at that time the laboratories were new in mental hospitals.[5]

By the mid-19th century, medicine was incorporating physics, chemistry and psychology to begin to explain mental illness in terms of disrupted nervous structure and function. Virchow had published his paper "Omnis Cellula e Cellula," which suggested that all pathology could be understood in terms of cellular disease. By the last half of the nineteen century, medical science became focused on the study of pathological anatomy and biochemical research was being conducted by prominent scientists.[6]

The American Medico-Psychological Association as it was called then, was celebrating its 50th anniversary about a year or so before I went to Westboro and S. Weir Mitchell, a famous neurologist of Philadelphia, had been the orator on that occasion. And he had brought the mental hospitals of the country to task saying that they were doing nothing in the actual study of mental diseases to advance it. There wasn't one of them that had a laboratory in the Institution –they were nothing but custodial institutions – they were just taking care of sick people and keeping them from running into each other, murdering and burning and getting into all sorts of mischief. They weren't any different from an alms house, except that patients were a little better taken care of. Well, that aroused considerable enthusiasm in all, particularly in this section of the country (in N.E.). So they all said we've got to have labs, you see, and labs became a fad.[7]

Fuller later attributed his interest in pursuing greater knowledge and a career in neuropathology and psychiatry to this address. Dr. Mitchell made many recommendations, which, at that time were considered revolutionary in the field of mental health. Among them were: the teaching of nurses about mental illness; the inclusion of training schools in mental hospitals; incorporating psychology and neurology in the preparation of doctors for the field of psychiatry; the removal of restraints in mental hospitals; and a greater awareness of the influence of heredity, marriage, environment, social pressures and race on mental illness. Perhaps his strongest attack on the treatment of mental disease and the one which had an impact on Fuller was the following:

> The question we ask at starting is if you, who are so powerful within these alien camps, are really doing all that might be done without serious increase of expenditure. Frankly speaking, we do not believe that you are so working these hospitals as to keep treatment or scientific precedent on the first line of medical advance. Where, we ask, are your annual reports of scientific study, of the psychology and pathology of your patients? They should be published apart...Believe me, the best hospitals of any kind are those where the most precise scientific work is done. There the treatment becomes accurate, the results best.[8]

Westboro State Hospital did not have a pathology laboratory at the time of Dr. Mitchell's speech in May, 1894. It wasn't until March, 1897 that the hospital appointed a pathologist, Dr. E. L. Mellis, to make microscopic examinations of the effects of mental disease upon the brain. In July 1897, Fuller began his appointment as an intern in the pathology laboratory at Westboro State Hospital.

> Work in another department of pathology has been furthered by the appointment of an interne [sic], whose whole time is given to the examination of pathological conditions in the living, taking up the work in this direction heretofore done by the assistant physicians; to which has been added, since April first, the examination of the blood of each patient admitted. While not expecting immediate results from the blood examinations, it is hoped that when a large number of cases have been collected they may be tabulated, and perhaps lead to valuable conclusions. Some interesting phenomena have already been observed, which, if verified later, will be given to the public.[9]

During his internship, Fuller developed an interest in the medical and neurological conditions of the psychiatric patients and was determined to learn what he could of the underlying deranged neuroanatomical pathology that caused what he had observed clinically. The scientific frame of reference for medical research had begun to shift from the study of the physiology and biochemistry of the living patient to postmortem pathology. In the United States, a sensitive moralizing society did not encourage the idea and practice of postmortem examination. Most American physicians had an aversion to autopsies and had not followed in this direction of European research in neurology. In Massachusetts, the legal position that covered postmortem practice by the medical profession had been defined and recognized by the state's medical society in 1894, but it was not adopted into law until 1911. Fuller voluntarily performed the unappealing and neglected task of post mortem examinations, and with technical assistance from nearby hospital laboratories, he learned how to make routine tissue sections and microscopic slides. He kept detailed records of the clinical histories and examinations of his autopsied cases.[10]

> Dr. Mellis who had been doing a lot of study in some of the fine laboratories in Europe came down to Boston. He was a Worcester man. He married a woman who was supposed to have considerable means so that although he'd been a good general practitioner, he had interested himself in neurology. He could afford to give some time to it. So he used to come out 2 or 3 times a week, take the autopsy material of the nervous system, brain and spinal cord and make anatomical studies of it, see what happened to these brains. Well he was not giving his full time to it – he wasn't even paid – he was interested, but he couldn't be called upon to urinalysis, blood counts, and go out and do the autopsies; leave his work in Boston where he was trying to build up a neurological service. Well I went out to be his helper, his striker, take care of the urinalysis, examine the sputum, see whether the patient had tuberculosis, make blood counts to see whether he was anemic, or not, and examine his stool to see whether he had any worm eggs or things of that sort.[11]

Fuller was so adept at his work, that, when Dr. Mellis left Westboro several months later to go to what was then the new Johns Hopkins Medical School in Baltimore to work with Professor Mahl in the anatomy department, he was appointed as the hospital's pathologist.

> ...one day [Dr. Mellis] suddenly announced that he was leaving and going down to Johns Hopkins. He packed up his things and left for Johns Hopkins. And there I was left with a lab on my hands. Along about the end of the year, I had been there 6 months, they appointed me the pathologist of the Westboro State Hospital. All of the other institutions were granted pathologists so they could say they had a lab and a pathologist....There was nobody more conscious of his inadequacy for that job than myself. Well I worked faithfully at that. I did autopsies and accumulated material but I didn't know the technique for working them up. Dr. Mellis hadn't been there long enough to show many of those techniques and I had to get them as best I could out of books and things of that sort, and they were pretty poor specimens of things.[12]

Despite his initial misgivings, Fuller soon demonstrated that he was more than capable of performing the work expected of him as the hospital's pathologist. He had passed his state medical board examinations and, in July 1898, received his license to practice medicine in Massachusetts. Fuller was intrigued by the newness of the neuropathology field and by the realization that he was one of the pioneers. "It was a time when it was popular to explore things in this area and I was one to begin."[13] His compelling sense was that through the laboratory, answers would be found to help unlock the mysteries of mental illness. In his first year at Westboro, Fuller published his findings on blood samples he had taken from mental patients upon admission to the hospital. Fuller's work did not go unrecognized by the hospital's superintendent. In his 1898 report to the hospital trustees, Dr. Adams included a six-page report describing Dr. Fuller's work and discoveries.[14] The report contained statistics which listed the number of laboratory procedures and some of the results. It also included documentation of his attempts to find significant data which might correlate with clinical syndromes. In one study reported, he collected and analyzed lab results of patients with diagnoses of mania, paranoia, melancholia, pernicious anemia (diseases common in the Westboro patient census) to see if there were any significant differences that should be explored. He looked for any possible influence of diabetes on mental illness, and began to study the urine of morphine and opium addicts to determine if there were any indicators which might be characteristic of the addiction. Finding some crystals in the urine of morphine addicts, Fuller documented his results and initiated a research project with Dr. Sutherland at Boston University to further investigate his findings.

Despite his achievements at Westboro, Fuller soon came face to face with the realities of institutional racism. While he had received an increase in his salary from $25 to $30 a month at the end of his first year, he learned that a young white physician, Dr. Baker, had recently joined the staff at a lesser rank at a starting salary of $50 a month.

> I was so furious I was just about ready to throw in the sponge, but Dr. Adams advised me not to do that. He said, 'You wouldn't get very far – perhaps you could stay here and you'd get to be an assistant superintendent, but there is not another mental hospital in this country that would make you superintendent of the hospital.' Now he said, 'You have shown considerable interest in neurological and pathological laboratories and trying to learn things about it and here's a new field and there's no telling how far you can go in that. In that field there would be least resistance – you'd be following the line of least resistance and you probably could make a name for yourself as a pathologist of some standing, whereas all you get to be – the best you could hope for – the way conditions are in the United States today, would be an assistant superintendent for the rest of your life.'[15]

Faced with the reality of his situation, Fuller realized that his choices were limited and agreed to stay on as pathologist at Westboro. He did, however, negotiate that in lieu of a raise, he be given two days a week to engage in other opportunities to pursue independent study and research. "Well, they were these old penny pinching New Englanders – why they could save $5 a month on it. Give him the two days a week – he is of no particular importance anyway. That is the way they reasoned. So they did."[16] The following year, he was offered an annual salary of $800 including six week's leave, providing he would agree to remain with the hospital for at least a year.

Fuller was beginning to distinguish himself in the field of neuropathology and in 1899, was appointed the Director of the Clinical Society Commission of Massachusetts. He devoted all his time to developing the pathology department, living on the grounds of the hospital and spending most of his waking hours in the laboratory. It was the custom during this time for state hospitals to furnish living quarters for staff physicians. His only relaxation was fishing in the large pond at the back of the hospital. His interest in the organic basis of mental disease led Fuller to focus his research on schizophrenia, manic-depressive psychosis, senility, and hereditary brain disease. As he studied and compared the Circle of Willis in various patients, he noted:

> In the way of histological investigation of the brain not much has been done, most of the time having been given to cases not yet fatal. More of this is hoped to be done later, as we recognize that such investigation will help much to give a better idea of the pathology of mental disease.[17]

During this time, the importance of dynamic factors in the development of mental disease and recognition of treatment led psychopathic hospitals to begin to develop collaborative relationships with universities and full-time academic positions in clinical medicine were being created. In the past, medical students had been taught by physicians who were in private practice. The majority of physicians had little education, having attended a course, a series of lectures, or, at most, a two-year medical program with an apprenticeship. The reform of medical education began during the period of good economy that occurred around 1870, fostered by endowments by wealthy patrons.[18] In 1899, two years after his graduation, Fuller was appointed to the faculty of his alma mater, the Boston University School of Medicine, as an instructor in pathology. He was one of the first black physicians to serve on the faculty of an American medical school other than Howard and Meharry. The American academic community was primarily a white population. Outside of black colleges and universities, black student enrollment was limited and faculties remained white. The consensus of white America at the turn of the century continued to be that blacks were inferior. During this period, science was often used in an attempt to prove the deficiency of persons of African descent. In 1900, the annual address at the meeting of the American Medico-Psychological Association reflected society's views on blacks.[19] Entitled "The Effect of Freedom Upon the Physical and Psychological Development of the Negro" and presented by Dr. J. Allison Hodes of Richmond, Virginia, it concluded that the Negro was "designed by

God and nature to remain a white man's servant, and must be kept in a condition of peonage and training until he acquired the qualities which he lacked."[20] Fuller later became a member of this organization and presented a pathology paper in 1912 at the annual meeting held in Atlantic City, New Jersey.

Although the appointment to a medical college carried a certain amount of prestige, Fuller's faculty appointment presented a new challenge. He would soon learn that with the position came a certain degree of compromise. Was he willing to suppress his views in order to follow the rules of the white academic institution and play the game? Or would he take a stand when necessary against prejudice and racism in academics and medicine? It wasn't long before an incident occurred during a medical faculty meeting that would test his convictions. The President of Boston University, in his address to the faculty, suggested that since Negroes constituted about 10 percent of the population of the United States, that the school make it a rule to limit the number of Negroes in the student body to one tenth.

> I was a little ashamed and somewhat disgusted by what had gone at the meeting. I wished I had not come to this thing – then when I got up to go out, I was sitting near the Dean and he said to me, 'I didn't hear you in this discussion' and I said, 'No, because I couldn't trust myself'. The President came up at the time and this was the remark I made to the Dean and the President of the University. Now, the President saw it was going pretty rough, and he said they didn't want to admit Negroes at all at first. Can you imagine that – that this free great University of thousands of students – a man making that sort of proposition – and the President of the University – and yet I suppose they made that again and again and even worse than that as far as that is concerned, I said 'Suppose here in the city of Boston you had said that only 10 percent of the student population of this University or whatever the percentage is, should be Irish, or should be Jews, how would that be accepted by the Irish or the Jewish population of Boston?[21]

Fuller's feelings about what had been said and how he should respond were complicated by his close relationship with the Dean of the medical school. In addition to befriending Fuller, the Dean had also consulted him for a personal medical problem. Although his first thought was to submit his resignation, he told the faculty that he would not resign.

> I said, "After such an exhibition as I have witnessed here, I think any of you would have resigned, but I'm not going to resign. I think it will serve as a little bit of inspiration to some colored youth at some time or other that might be really worthwhile.' I did not and that was the only reason. How I restrained myself I couldn't to this day explain. Except that I must have been guided by some kind of genius or good angel or good spirit. But as I look back on it now, I think I won by not resigning.[22]

It wasn't long before Fuller felt the need to move beyond the routine of the laboratory at Westboro in order to advance his technical skills in the accelerating field of histopathology. During the winter months of 1900, Fuller took a leave of absence from Westboro and went to study at the Carnegie Institute, which was affiliated with the New York University School of Medicine and located in a large office building in New York City.

> The director's tenure was then in doubt and although he welcomed me, I felt the atmosphere was too rarefied for me. They spoke a psychological, anthropological and metaphysical anatomical language which was beyond me. So I repaired to the pathological lab of Edward K. Dunham.[23]

Edward K. Dunham, Professor of Pathology at New York's Belleview Hospital Medical College, was a leading pathologist and associate of Hermann Biggs, a close friend of William Henry Welch at Johns Hopkins, Christian A. Herter (who had proposed Dunham for Board membership in the founding of the Rockefeller Institute), and other notable professionals. He had spent time in Germany undertaking advanced study in the laboratories of Robert Koch and other prominent reseachers.[24] In Dunham's laboratory, Fuller had the opportunity to learn more about the histopathology of the human body and to perform autopsies in the morgue at Bellevue Hospital.

For the next three years following his return to Westboro, Fuller worked to establish a closer relationship between the laboratory and the ward service. He began making regular rounds on the wards with the clinical psychiatrist and invited the psychiatrist to spend some time in his laboratory. In the past, both public and private institutions in Massachusetts had only provided custodial care to the mentally ill. The hospital had begun to move away from the established model of psychiatric care in 1898, erecting the first building in the Massachusetts state hospitals for the exclusive care of the acute insane and creating a psychopathic department. The two-story building, with separate wings for men and women, contained suites for physicians and administrators, electric shock treatment, and examining rooms. The program was based on the idea that some psychiatric patients could be rehabilitated and returned to the community. Only those patients with the potential for discharge were considered for admission. Under the direction of Dr. Henry Klopp, the program featured innovations in treatment such as open-air therapy, where verandas were used to promote sleep, appetite, and assimilation; neutral baths, used as a sedative in calming agitation and controlling depression; and work-training, which employed patients in various departments of the hospital (laundry, greenhouse, building repairs) to develop skills that would prepare them to re-enter the community.

In his annual report to the hospital trustees in 1900, Fuller had indicated the inclusion of laboratory tests as part of hospital procedure and had shared his vision of the laboratory as an integral component in the treatment of mental illness.

> During the year just completed, the greater portion of the time has been devoted to work of a purely clinical nature. The improved facilities for work of this character has made the laboratory more than ever an adjunct to the ward

work of the clinical physicians. If for no other reason than this, I think the laboratory justifies its raison d'etre. Work in the line of research is certainly to be desired. It is in this way a better knowledge of the causes that operate against mental equilibrium is largely to be acquired – an acquisition which eventually must have a salutary effect on the body politic, and result either in a diminution proportionately of insanity or lead to effective measures of prophylaxis in many cases. I regret no work in the line of pure research has been done this year.[25]

Realizing the importance of documenting the results of his research and the contribution that such research could make to the science of mental illness, Fuller began to write up his findings. He became the editor of the *Westboro State Hospital Papers*, a publication which reported the scientific work of the hospital staff.

By 1902, Fuller had published a paper in the *New England Medical Gazette* and had completed two more papers for publication. In his characteristically modest way, he introduced the hospital and its trustees to one of his inventions, an apparatus that made photomicrographs of slides, in his annual report.

It has always been our object to keep full records of all specimens which have come to the laboratory. This year, with the aid of a simple apparatus constructed from odds and ends, the microscopical records have been enhanced by the introduction of the photomicrograph.[26]

In October, 1903, the hospital's Board of Trustees voted to increase Fuller's annual salary to $1200, a significant amount when compared to the average physician's yearly income of $750.[27] Fuller's expanding role at Westboro was instrumental in the hospital trustees' decisions to approve better accommodations for his laboratory. In 1901, they had voted to approve $5000 for a new pathological building and to authorize the purchase of "needed apparatus for the pathological department at a cost not exceeding $50", and in August 1904, the Board reported, "removal of pathologist to Ward Fourteen and the construction of a tinned door between that and the administration side."[28]

When he was not working in his lab at Westboro or teaching at Boston University, Fuller spent his time reading. From 1902 through 1906, he recorded his book purchases in a small brown notebook. The list of titles contained a variety of topics and interests and included books on fishing, bookbinding (a passionate hobby in his later years), the poetry of Keats and Milton, the plays of George Bernard Shaw, Latin and Greek classics, and German. There were many months when Fuller spent more than his salary of $20 - $30 on books and bookbinding.[29]

It was during this time that Fuller began a friendship with Mary (May) Bragg, a nurse at Westboro. The two soon found that they shared a love of Latin and began going on weekend retreats, along with May's brother, Evan Bragg, to the family's farm in Sidney, Maine. While at the farm, they would read Latin for three or four days at a time. The friendship would endure throughout their lifetimes. The question of whether or not there was ever more than friendship between Solomon and May, who was white, was posed many years later by his son, Solomon, Jr.

> The friendship that developed was about as precious as it could get. They became the dearest of friends. People would be tempted to write of a romance between them.[30]

Fuller's enthusiasm for learning and the influence of Edward Dunham led him to consider the advantages of going abroad for post graduate studies in neuroscience research. Shortly after his return to Westboro from his studies in Dunham's laboratory, Fuller began to save his earnings in order to pursue additional education and training in neuropathology and psychiatry with the leading experts in Europe.

Beginning in the late 1800s, it was not uncommon for many prestigious physicians to go to Europe for training that was not available in the United States until many years later. In his address at the opening of the Rockefeller Institute in 1906, L. Emmett Holt stated: "Five years ago there was in France, Germany, England, Russia and Japan well-equipped and endowed institutions for research in medicine. In this country not one existed."[31] The lack of teaching and research institutions and laboratories for advanced learning in the medical sciences in the United States was in large measure due to the compelling need for the medical profession to care for the sick. In the developing country, what Benjamin Franklin called "...the drudgery of setting new colonies which confines the attention of people to mere necessities" left little or no energy or funds for the luxury of institutions of advanced learning or research.[32]

Impressed by the scientific study of mental disease in Germany and the high quality of its institutions of learning, Fuller requested a leave of absence from Westboro to pursue post graduate education at the University of Munich. He had heard of the innovative research and treatment approaches being implemented by Emil Kraepelin at the university's new psychiatric clinic and had written to his former mentor, Dr. Mellis at Johns Hopkins in Baltimore, inquiring about Kraepelin's work.

In a letter dated April 20, 1904, Dr. Mellis replied:

> I don't think you could spend time with a better man. I was much impressed with the character of the clinics in Psychiatry...That is just now the mecca of Americans interested in the study of insanity. This marks the opening of a very important era in medicine, and its relevance to psychiatry may be closer than we think.[33]

In April 1904, the hospital's Board of Trustees voted "that Dr. Fuller shall have six months leave of absence beginning at his convenience in the autumn for study in pathology and that this leave shall be with half pay."[34] Shortly before Fuller's departure to Germany, the Trustees voted to grant him an additional two months leave without pay, reporting that "Dr. Coles is now ready to do Dr. Fuller's work...."[35]

His journey into the advanced study of neurological science was about to begin.

Chapter Five

The Science of Germany
Munich
1904

The universities of Germany are her chief glory, and the greatest boon she can give us in the New World is to return our young men infected with the spirit of earnestness and with the love of thoroughness which characterizes the work done in them.

William Osler, 1890[1]

It was in Germany where Fuller would learn to perfect the techniques of medical research and investigation inspired by the abundance of clinical material and the availability of private instruction by great teachers. His trip to Germany would remain the highlight of Fuller's life as evidenced by his letters and interviews in later years.

While en route to Germany, Fuller traveled to Africa to visit his mother, whom he had not seen since his departure for America. His family had continued to maintain positions of political power, and at the time of Fuller's visit, his cousin, Sara, was the wife of Arthur Barclay, President of Liberia. This was the last time that Fuller would set foot in his homeland.

I was home for two weeks and I took a boat, a Spanish steamer from Monrovia and we stopped at the Canaries for a day and then on to Cadiz where we went into dry-dock for about a week. So that gave me an opportunity to see something of Cadiz and that part of Spain and after the bottom of the boat had been scraped and the dry-dock filled we sailed out. We passed the Straits of Gibraltar and saw the great Rock, just as it is pictured in the Prudential Life

> Insurance Company advertisements. But opposite Gibraltar was another prominent point on the African side, the Sierra Leone Mountains and I rather liked that I think better... Well, in due time we were in the Mediterranean, and from the Mediterranean we sailed through to Barcelona, where I spent a few days and then took a train to Paris. A few days in Paris and then on the train to Munich. I arrived in Munich, I think it was a Sunday evening.[2]

Fuller's first impression of Munich was influenced by the fact that his arrival coincided with the city's celebration of *die Tollen Tage* (the Crazy Days). The German equivalent of Rio's Carnivale or New Orleans' Mardi Gras, the occasion is marked by dressing up in costumes and festivities that go on for days.

> I arrived at the hotel there, called the Reichshoff, there was rather gay goings on there, some private parties – there were a lot of private parties during that season, they were held on Sunday with big celebrations on Wednesday and Saturday night for the general public but the little intimate parties were usually on Sunday night and were rather gay and I thought to myself, if this is what Munich is like, I'm going to have a really great time here.[3]

Shortly after his arrival in Munich, Fuller became ill with influenza. Although he was discouraged that his ill health would keep him from beginning his studies for several days, he was pleasantly surprised by the treatment he received, and by the warm hospitality and concern that he experienced. Social status in Germany was not measured by a man's income, but by his title or occupation. Those holding doctoral degrees were addressed as *Herr Doktor*.

> I couldn't get out to go to the clinic or anything of that sort. I sent for a doctor, he came in to see me twice. A young practitioner, and when he was through, I asked him for his bill and well, he was astounded or appeared to be at any rate that I should ask him for a bill to treat a Herr Colleague. To accept a fee from a Herr Colleague was unthinkable.[4]

The advances in science during the previous century had resulted in a separation, yet coexistence of science and religion. In Europe, neurologists had begun to group neurological symptoms into diseases and neuropathologists were identifying the pathology to explain these clinical phenomena. The school of pathological physiology, which emphasized laboratory research, had developed in Germany during the late 1800s. German physicians objected to the anatomical approach in medicine, maintaining that what was observed in the autopsy was only the end result of a pathological process, not the process itself.[5] Under the German model of medical education, a medical school must be part of a university, with basic sciences taught in liberal arts departments. The school must have its own departments for the biomedical sciences to encourage research, and clinical instruction should be provided in a teaching hospital with full-time faculty staff. At the urging of Adolf von Harnack, the famous theologian, the Kaiser established an institute for basic research.

With the opening of the Munich Psychiatric Hospital, the relationship between the asylum and the university encouraged and facilitated research in the organic conception of insanity. The research institute (now known as the Max Planck Institute of Psychiatry) became a model for many psychiatric research facilities throughout the world. Emil Kraepelin, regarded as an influential German psychiatrist, held the Chair of Psychiatry at the University of Munich. A pioneer in experimental psychology and psycho-physiological research, Kraepelin, along with his colleagues, Alois Alzheimer, Otto Bollinger, Karl Weiler, Karl von Voit, Eduard Reiss, and Felix Plaut, were responsible for the basis of psychiatric epidemiology and psychiatric genetics.

> I went out to see Professor Kraepelin at the new clinic there which had been open only a short while – had an interview with Kraepelin who I learned later spoke perfect English. At the time I wasn't particularly impressed with him. I was concerned with getting in and he was rather a distant sort of fellow, entirely impersonal, but he told me to go see the clinic and to the pursers office, and he gave me a card indicating that I had permission to attend his clinical lectures.[6]

In addition to attending Kraepelin's lectures and clinic, Fuller was soon following him on "ward walks". It was in the wards of the psychiatric hospital, that he was able to observe Kraepelin's methods for reducing the use of physical restraints to calm agitated patients, such as frequent baths, narcoleptics, and tranquilizers.[7]

Fuller had studied the German language before leaving for Germany, learning the language sufficiently well enough to follow lectures and clinical demonstrations.

While working under Kraepelin, he learned a new classification system that facilitated the diagnosis and treatment of mental diseases. Kraepelin's utilization of the medical approach of detailed observation, careful description and organization of data, as well as his concern for the patients would influence Fuller's practice of psychiatry when he returned to the United States.

Fuller registered for two semesters at the University of Munich. Taking advantage of the university's distinguished faculty, he attended autopsy lectures given by Otto Bollinger, a pathologist, and Hans Schmaus' lectures on the anatomy of the spinal cord.

> ...I went over to the Pathological Institute which was across the street and took some courses in general pathology and this Professor Bollinger, who was a rather prominent pathologist in Munich at the time and there was a wealth of material from the various morgues and the hospitals there every morning for his lecture and almost every conceivable sort of disease you could find in autopsy was demonstrated at these meetings. At the same time I went to see a comparatively young man, Schmaus was his name, and I'd been familiar with some of his writings and he gave special lectures on the spinal cord, so I took his course, it was very nearly over then and he was closing up for the spring

semester and I wanted to continue working with him and he saw that I was particularly interested in the pathology of the brain itself...[8]

It was Hans Schmaus who sent Fuller to Alois Alzheimer, the director of the histopathological laboratory at the university. As a result of his interview with Alzheimer, Fuller was one of five students admitted to the "privalesmus," the course offered by Alzheimer.

> I went there to see Alzheimer and there was a reception room filled with men who wanted to take his course in the pathology of the brain and apparently all young men who were recently graduated and he called them by turn to see what they wanted and he turned each of them down as being *'nichtreif genug'* as he called it, not ripe enough. They had just graduated from the University and I thought if he was turning Germans down like that, I wouldn't have a ghost of a show. So when it became my turn, I was the last one, he smiled and said, 'Herr Colleague, what can I do for you?' And I told him I wanted to take his course. He said, 'you know my course is very strictly limited, when the number is five, we cannot take any more than five and it all depends upon your experience. Have you had any experience in working among the insane?' I said, yes, I had been at the Massachusetts State Hospital for the Insane for a period of about 6 years. He said, 'do you know how to cut and mount brain tissue because we can't teach the men those fundamentals.' I said yes, I worked in the laboratory practically all that period and I spent some time with Dr. Edward Dunham in New York at the Carnegie Institute, and he smiled and said 'that University is President Warren's University, isn't it?' Warren was President at the time, at least he was president when I was there and apparently he knew Dr. Warren and he said to report at 9 o'clock in the morning.[9]

Located on the third floor of the psychiatric hospital, Alzheimer's laboratory was a large, sparsely furnished room that contained six benches with equipment for conducting neuropathological research. Germany's progress in pathology was advanced by the construction of better microscopes and the development of histology, a technique that hardened body tissues, embedding them in rigid materials to facilitate cutting, slicing them into thin sections, and coloring them with stains which contrasted the cellular elements. Using the new laboratory techniques and experimental methods developed by Alzheimer and his colleagues, the research assistants examined brain and spinal cord tissue. The aim of Alzheimer's staff was to demonstrate and prove anatomical relationships to mental illness associated with general paresis, senile dementia, arteriosclerosis, and some forms of luetic infection and psychoses against the generally accepted functional causes.[10] Visiting scholars and students who had been privileged to work in Alzheimer's laboratory in Munich recalled that he was a dedicated teacher.[11] Alzheimer was always accessible to his students and, being an incessant cigar smoker it was recalled that there was a cigar butt left on each student's bench at the end of the day.

Alzheimer was a delightful sweet character, unassuming, very unassuming, and the poorest lecturer I ever heard. He used to lecture for the big clinics. But when he sat down at your desk and gave you an hour while you talked with him at weekly seminars at the clinic and at the little suppers that followed later; that's where you learned the stuff. He was so self-conscious when he was speaking, you know, I don't see how anyone could learn anything from him. But he was generous, very kindly, a rather big man, with large hands and you wondered that he could manipulate things so well. He certainly could. Wonderful character.[12]

Like most of his fellow American students, Fuller worked hard and seriously and had little time outside of the laboratory for a social life. He was amazed by the productivity of his German colleagues, despite the fact that they never worked long hours and always took time off to celebrate the country's many holidays. Fuller did not find his skin color to be a barrier to social relationships in Germany, and close and enduring friendships were formed in the laboratory. One of Fuller's colleagues and companions during this time was Frederich H. Lewy, who later became known for his research in Parkinson's disease and who discovered the characteristic neuronal bodies named after him.[13]

One of the patients being treated by Alzheimer during this time was the famous first identified case of what would later be labeled as Alzheimer's disease. Auguste D., as she was known, had been institutionalized with symptoms of dementia when she was in her late forties and was observed by Alzheimer over the course of her progressive illness. In the early stages of her illness, she exhibited changes in her personality with strong feelings of jealousy toward her husband. As the illness progressed, her memory became impaired, she became increasingly paranoid that people were trying to kill her, and she no longer was oriented to her surroundings.

In 1906, four and one-half years after her initial symptoms appeared, Auguste D. died in an institution in a fetal position at age 51.[14]

Alzheimer's original file on Auguste D. was found in 1995 in the archives of the Department of Psychiatry and Psychotherapy at the Johann Wolfgang Goethe University in Frankfort[15] In his notes, Alzheimer documented his examination findings, which included the inability of the patient to identify and remember objects, as well as changes in her handwriting. An autopsy conducted on August D. revealed excessive atrophy of the brain and neurofibrillary tangles and sclerotic plaques leading Alzheimer to speculate that this was a distinct type of dementia with unique clinical and anatomical characteristics. Prior to this case, the plaques found in Auguste D.'s brain had only been noted in aged, senile patients and not in association with the neurofibrillary tangles in younger demented patients.

Alzheimer's findings were first presented at a meeting of the South-West German Alienists in 1906 and later published in several German journals in 1907. In 1910, the dementia identified by Alzheimer was given the name

"Alzheimer's disease" by Kraepelin in the eighth edition of his book, *Psychiatrie*.[16]

Little is known about Fuller's work in Alzheimer's laboratory. Those who undertook assistantships or graduate studies in Germany became more or less invisible during their time spent in hospitals and laboratories. As an assistant to a well-known researcher, they became subordinates, and although they supported and carried out the research of their chiefs and even contributed new ideas and innovative skills that improved the production in the laboratory and enhanced his reputation, they received little or no credit for their efforts. The chief usually enjoyed full credit for innovations and discoveries made by members of his research team.

Alzheimer was the only neuropathologist in his laboratory, and as he did not have funding to support his work, he had to depend upon his students to carry out his research. This proved to be an advantageous situation for the students who, under Alzheimer's mentorship, had to perform all of the basic laboratory work and in doing so, contributed much to the fundamentals of brain research skills.[17] With Fuller's enthusiasm for learning, his self-taught skills, as well as those skills learned under the direction of Edward K. Dunham, one can only imagine the important contributions that he made to the research being conducted in Munich. He had probably examined more brain specimens than anyone in Alzheimer's laboratory with the possible exception of the Director himself. The influence of Alzheimer's research on the neuropathology of dementing illnesses is apparent in Fuller's later work on Alzheimer's disease.

Before leaving Germany, Fuller stopped in Frankfort to visit the Senckenberg Institute where the noted scientist, Carl Weigert, had conducted his research on tissue repair. A professor of pathology, Weigert was known for the development of the specific myelin sheath stain that helped to improve studies of the anatomy and pathology of the nervous system. Weigert had died the previous year and his laboratory had been made a shrine. It was there that Fuller met Ludwig Edinger, a psychiatrist who was involved in the development of research on the structure of the central nervous system.

> There was a man there who had succeeded to the laboratory. He was the head of the Journal of Pathology and he was very nice and it was there he introduced me to Edinger and others down there that I had known. And when I was about to leave he said, 'of course, you are going to see Ehrlich.' I said no, I have no business with Ehrlich, although I know of nothing that would give me greater pleasure than to have an introduction to him. 'Oh', he said, 'you don't need an introduction. Go see him anyway, he'll be glad to see you.'[18]

Dr. Paul Ehrlich, a cousin of Carl Weigert, was the Director of the Imperial Institute for Chemical Research. An immunologist who was a leading advocate for chemical and experimental pathology, Ehrlich made important contributions to several new areas of medical science including immunology, hematology, and chemotherapy.

...and I went, but he happened to be at a meeting of some sort, but I was shown into his waiting room and I found there another man – he was a young American. So we had been sitting there about 5 minutes when Ehrlich bounded into the room. He's one of those pretty important fellows, you know, and he got into the door and he asked who's first, in German, and this fellow didn't move, so I responded and pointed to that fellow over there. So he went over to this man and he had so little knowledge of German and Ehrlich had so little knowledge of English that they couldn't make themselves understood. This fellow was trying to say to him that he'd like to come to work with him in his laboratory during the summer. Ehrlich was trying to tell him he had shut down in the summer and was going away on his vacation, but if he came back in the fall he would be glad to have him. Finally in desperation he turned to me and asked if I could help him out. I was pretty well along with my German by that time and I straightened them out. At any rate he learned that the man had come from Professor Vaughn's laboratory – this fellow's name was Edmonds if I remember correctly. He told Edmonds that it wouldn't be of any advantage to work there because there wouldn't be anything going on at that time except the routine work of the laboratory and he wouldn't be there until the fall. Then he invited us to see the Institute. And he took us around personally. He had to attend a meeting of Trustees or something of that sort and he said 'I want you gentlemen to see the new Institute.' Ehrlich called one of his assistants, a young man by the name of Schmidt, who conducted us over the new institute which was only a short distance from the old building – there we were shown all over the building. We must have spent about an hour on that little jaunt – after that was over we prepared to take our leave and the young Doctor suggested we go see Ehrlich because 'he had requested that you call to see him after you had seen the new building.' So we went over. Ehrlich was at leisure then – he conducted us into his private office – took out a box of cigars – cocked his feet on the top of the desk and began to talk. He talked about everything for four hours, it seemed, concerning medicine and what each of us had hoped to do in our fields. A very encouraging talk. He treated us as though he had known us all his life or all of our lives or as though we were children of intimate friends of his. We then, in due season, left him, thanking him, showed our appreciation of him and of so much time, and made our departure.[19]

As Ehrlich accompanied the men through the gate that led from the laboratory to the sidewalk, he asked them if they knew of anyone who was coming to the United States. He had a small package of mice he wanted taken to Dr. W.T. Councilman at the Harvard Medical School in Boston. Fuller offered to carry the mice to the laboratory at Harvard, since he was sailing for the United States that week.

Ehrlich agreed and had the package delivered to Fuller on board the ship, the S.S. Lucania shortly before it left Liverpool on July 29. From those mice, a pair of white mice that had been infected with tumor cells, and their offspring came the research on the histology of cancer by Dr. Ernest Tyzzer, which was later published in the *Journal for Medical Research.*

Fuller would remember those two days spent in Frankfort as "golden and glorious", and "that afternoon with Ehrlich was worth a college education – a gracious, friendly man".[20] His friendship with Paul Ehrlich, who was to receive the Nobel Prize in Medicine in 1908 for his work in immunity, continued until Ehrlich's death in 1915.

1. Anna Ursala James Fuller

2. Solomon Carter Fuller

3. Westboro Insane Hospital

4. Psychiatric clinic at the Ludwig-Maximilians University, Munich, Germany, 1904

5. Dr. Alois Alzheimer and students in Alzheimer's laboratory (Fuller is seated to the left of Alzheimer), 1905

Frankfurt a/M., 26.Juli,1905

Sehr geehrter Herr Kollege!

Ich habe von Ihrer freundlichen
Erlaubnis Gebrauch gemacht und Ihnen gestern, also am
25., abends, 3,Mäuschen in einem Käfig an das Schiff
geschickt. Ich wollte Sie bitten, nach der Ankunft
gleich anzusehen, ob die Tiere noch am Leben sind,
was ich sicher voraussetze, und ihnen gleich etwas
feuchtes Brot zu reichen, sowie sie auch unterwegs gut
zu halten.

Ich denke, dass Sie keinerlei Mühe durch de
Transport haben werden, durch den Sie meinem Freunde,
Herrn Professor Councilman und auch mir einen grossen G
fallen thun.

Indem ich Ihnen eine recht gute Reise
wünsche, bin ich mit besten Empfehlungen und in vor-
züglicher Hochachtung, sowie mit nochmaligem Danke
für Ihre Freundlichkeit,

Ihr sehr ergebener

Herrn Dr. Salomon Fuller,
    S.S. "Lucania", in Ausfahrt,
    Cunard Line, Liverpool.

6. Letter to Fuller from Paul Ehrlich confirming arrangements for Fuller to carry mice
from Prof. Ehrlich's laboratory to the United States to be used for research, 1905

7. Solomon Carter Fuller

8. Mary (May) Bragg Weston

9. Fuller (last row, far right) is among the group of scientists invited to celebrate Clark University's 20th Anniversary

10. Fuller family on front steps of Solomon and Meta's home in Framingham, Massachusetts, 1944. (Front row: son Solomon, Jr., grandson John, Meta, grandson Robert, daughter-in-law Marie. Second row: son Thomas, daughter-in-law Harriet, grandson Solomon III, grandson Thomas, Jr. Back row: son Perry.)

11. Solomon and Meta

H. H. WALKER, M. D., PRESIDENT
NASHVILLE, TENNESSEE

ARMEN G. EVANS, M. D., PRESIDENT-ELECT
CLEVELAND, OHIO

March 7, 1950

Dr. Solomon C. Fuller
31 Warren Road
Framingham, Massachusetts

My dear Dr. Fuller:

It was certainly nice to get your note of February 20th with reference to the announcement of the 38th annual meeting of the John A. Andrew Clinic, April 2-7.

We shall always remember the very fine part that you had in training there in Boston the original group of psychiatrists that came to start the Veterans Hospital at Tuskegee. Of that original group, Tildon, Branche, and Davis are still here, Tildon and Branche occupying the two highest positions in the hospital, Davis heading the Department of Physical Medicine and the only Diplomate of the American Board of Physical Medicine that we have in our group. The other member of the group, S. O. Johnson, is now head of the State Institution at Lakin, West Virginia. He, too, is a Diplomate of the American Board. It certainly must make you feel very proud to know that you had a great deal to do with the training of these young men who have done so much in the field in which you started them off.

You certainly will be interested to know now since all your life you were connected with a teaching institution and are in a position to know just what that means to an institution, that the Veterans Hospital now has a residency program for the training of young physicians in surgery and internal medicine. We hope soon to start one in psychiatry and neurology. In this effort we have an affiliation with the University of Alabama's Medical College and Emory University Medical College in Atlanta, Georgia. This year at our Clinic we are going to have a day in psychiatry at which time we are having Walter Freeman of Washington, Daniel Blain, Medical Director of the American Psychiatric Association, and others to come and talk to our men on what the general practitioner should know about psychiatry. We believe that this will be a great addition to the training of physicians and surgeons in the South.

We hope that you can come down to visit us again. We can assure you that in opening the psychiatric meeting this year, you will be given due credit for the tremendously fine part that you played in the starting and the development of this great work so closely allied and associated with the work of Dr. Washington, the founder of Tuskegee Institute.

With sincere best regards to you and your family,

Sincerely yours,

EUGENE H. DIBBLE, JR., M. D.
Medical Director

EHD/mk

12. Letter acknowledging Fuller's contribution to the training of medical staff at Tuskegee Institute, 1950

13. The Dr. Solomon Fuller Mental Health Center, Boston

by Morrie Turner

14. *Boston Sunday Globe* cartoon featuring Fuller, 1976

𝔉uller 𝔐iddle 𝔖chool

Framingham School Committee
Cordially Invites You to Attend The Dedication Of
The Fuller Middle School

Illustrated By Marc Fuller and Robert Fuller

15. Invitation to the dedication of the Fuller Middle School, 1995

16. Solomon Carter Fuller, Jr. and his second wife, Grace

Chapter Six

The Doctor and the Sculptor
Westboro
1906

> Dr. S.C. Fuller, our pathologist, was absent from the hospital from November, 1904 to August 1905, going to Munich, Germany, and having an opportunity while there, of studying under Kraepelin. He returns to the hospital with well-earned knowledge and increased interest in his work.[1]

Upon his return to the United States, Fuller resumed his duties as pathologist at Westboro Insane Hospital and his teaching at Boston University Medical School. While he was studying in Germany, plans had been underway to build the hospital's new pathology laboratory that he had designed prior to leaving for Europe.

> We note with special satisfaction that the new pathological building is nearly completed, and we feel that it will be of great service to the hospital. The pathological work for some years has been of a high order, and has deserved better accommodations than any previously furnished; and the new building, with the work rooms it contains, will make possible still better work, both a routine nature and also original investigation into a new and unknown field of medicine.[2]

The country that Fuller returned to in 1905 had seen little change in the way in which its black population was treated. The widely accepted black stereotypes usually remained unchallenged during this period and racial segregation continued to be enforced in housing and employment, with little or no systematic rebuttal from the country's black intellectuals. In 1901, W.E.B. DuBois had voiced his opposition to the teachings of Booker T. Washington, which, according to DuBois, accepted the alleged inferiority of the Negro as part of an agreement for limited advancement. He then began to assemble a small group of African Americans, known as the Talented Tenth, who were dedicated to self-determination, higher education, and the right to vote for blacks.[3] Three months prior to Fuller's return to the United States, the Niagara Movement was formed in Niagara Falls, Canada, under the leadership of DuBois to work towards full citizenship for Negroes.

Upon returning to his duties at Westboro and to his teaching at the medical school, Fuller found that there were still very few opportunities for blacks in the fields of science and medicine. Obtaining funding to support his scientific research proved to be a major obstacle for Fuller, as foundations and other funding sources could not envision blacks engaging in pure science. While he continued to teach pathology and neurology courses as an instructor in the Department of Neurology and Psychiatry at Boston University Medical School, the white academic environment remained unwilling to accept Fuller as an equal in its faculty ranks and he was never officially put on the payroll. He drew a small salary for his teaching, receiving twenty-four dollars a month, compared to twenty-eight dollars a month for other instructors.

With the new pathology building completed in 1906, Fuller was eager to put to use the new scientific knowledge and skills he had learned in the German laboratories. The experience of working in a well-equipped laboratory in an atmosphere that was stimulating and competitive provided the impetus to develop his own research interests and to focus on publishing his findings. Immersed in his research and teaching, Fuller had little time for a social life. One day, while working at Westboro, he was visited by a young artist, Meta Vaux Warrick, who was staying with a friend in Boston who had told her about the accomplished young doctor. He gave her a tour of his laboratory and she suggested that he use his knowledge and equipment to pursue photography. He followed her advice and began a hobby that he continued for most of his life. For the remaining three months of Meta's stay in Boston, the two were inseparable, going to the theater and exploring the city.

> He says he fell in love with me at that visit at Westboro State Hospital. That's what he claims. I had a mass of hair, then. I wouldn't call him a handsome man. Depends on what you call handsome. He was fairly tall and thin. He proposed to me the Sunday before I left. I had told him I felt it wasn't quite fair, that I had not lived a satisfactory life. My Aunt pulling me one way (she was financing me some); my mother was pulling me another way (she was financing me, of course), and then I was helping her in the hairdressing parlor. I was a disappointment to them because I wasn't making money hand-over-fist. I was eager to get out of that rut, away from that contest between my aunt and my mother.[4]

By the time that Meta Vaux Warrick met Solomon Carter Fuller, she had already established herself as a talented sculptor. Born into a wealthy black family in Philadelphia on June 9, 1877, she was reported to be a descendant of an Ethiopian princess brought to the United States as a slave. Meta's father, William H. Warrick, had been a barber who later, with her maternal grandfather, Henry Jones, became one of Philadelphia's most celebrated caterers who served mostly white customers. During the mid-nineteenth century, blacks dominated both the catering and hair cutting businesses in Philadelphia. A former slave from Virginia, Henry Jones was a well known member of the trade guild of caterers that "transformed the Negro cook and waiter into the public caterer and restaurateur, and raised a crowd of underpaid menials to become a set of self-reliant, original business men, who amassed fortunes for themselves and won general respect for their people."[5] Meta's father and grandfather served many of the wealthy families of Philadelphia, New Jersey, and New York and in 1860, they catered the banquet given at the Philadelphia Academy of Music for the Prince of Wales. When Henry Jones died in 1875, his funeral procession was turned away from the predominately white Mt. Moriah Cemetery despite the fact that before his death, he had paid for a cemetery plot. His title to the plot was eventually confirmed by the courts.

Meta's mother, Emma Jones Warrick, was a beautician whose customers were upper-class white women. Meta was named for one of her mother's customers, who was the daughter of U.S. Congressman Richard Vaux of Pennsylvania. The youngest of three children, Meta led a sheltered life as a child, with limited contact with other black children due to the fact that her parents wanted her to grow up to be like the ladies who came to her mother's beauty salon. She spent her childhood summers in Atlantic City where her parents owned several barber and hairdressing shops. She remembers those summers as being one of her first experiences with racial prejudice. Atlantic City prohibited black children and white children from playing together, so in order for her to swim with her white playmates, they had to go to the beach early in the morning when there were few people on the beach. On Sundays, her family would drive to Ventnor, a small town south of Atlantic City, where there was a beach and bathhouse designated for blacks. Prohibited from riding on the boardwalk's carousel, Meta would stand and watch her friends as they went up and down on the horses to the music of *The Poet and Peasant*. For the remainder of her life, she would associate the melody with being unwanted and rejected. Years later, while playing the guitar at a concert in Philadelphia, she refused to join the other members of her guitar and mandolin club in playing the piece which was on the program.

> ...Well, I hated it so, I had not been able to bring myself to learn to play the music. I held my guitar and went through the motions. The director noticed I wasn't playing and winked his eye at me, but nobody else knew the difference.[6]

As a young child, Meta was introduced to the world of art by her father and her sister. Her father would often take her to the Philadelphia Academy of Fine Arts where he would explain the paintings and sculpture to her. Her sister, Blanche, who was a talented painter and sculptor, would give her bits of clay and other art materials to play with. Meta's brother and grandfather contributed to her fascination with horror by telling her endless horror stories. The horror themes expressed in her later work earned her the title of "the sculptor of horrors".[7] Meta continued her drawing and sculpting while attending the Philadelphia black segregated public schools. At age 12, she was selected to attend J. Liberty Tadd, an art school that held classes one day a week for students selected from Philadelphia schools. At the school, children were taught free-hand drawing in elementary design, clay modeling, and wood carving. Upon graduation, she was encouraged by one of her art teachers to apply for a three-year scholarship to the Philadelphia School of Industrial Art, which later became the Pennsylvania College of Art. In the art contest held to determine the scholarship winner, Meta won the top prize given among the twenty competitors. During her student years at the art school, she began to focus on sculpture and won many honors in the Philadelphia art community. All students receiving scholarships were required to produce some work that represented the school's focus. Meta's bas-relief frieze, *The Procession of Arts and Crafts*, was made up of thirty-seven figures dressed in medieval costumes in a procession. The piece won the twenty-five-dollar prize for the best work in modeling for the year. When Meta completed her three years of study at the Philadelphia School of Industrial Art in 1896, she was awarded a graduate fellowship. The following year, her teachers urged her to go to Paris for postgraduate study under France's master sculptors. Her father had recently died and her mother was reluctant to let her go, so Meta postponed her trip, working in her mother's beauty shop while continuing to develop her artistic talent.

With the encouragement and support of her family, friends, and teachers, Meta sailed for Europe aboard the *Belgianland* on September 30, 1899, stopping in England where she spent a month with Harriet Loudin, a friend of her mother and the wife of Frederick Loudin, director of the Fisk Jubilee Singers. Arriving in Paris by train on October 26, Meta looked around the station's crowded waiting room for her uncle's friend, Henry O. Tanner, a noted black artist, who had promised to meet her. After waiting for several hours, she realized that Henry Tanner was not coming and set off by taxi for the American Art Student's Club for Women, often referred to as the American Girl's Club, where she had been promised a room at a reasonable rate. She arrived at the Club in the early morning, hungry and tired. The reception that she received proved to be a traumatic experience that left a permanent scar on Meta's memory. Sixty years after the incident, she was able to recount much of the conversation that took place. The director of the Club, Miss Acley, who was seated in front of a vanity mirror having her hair styled by her maid, looked up with a smile when Mlle. Warrick was announced. Meta seated herself in a pink satin chair directly behind Miss Acley and raised the veil of her hat, revealing her face. Instantly the director's smile disappeared as she caught a glimpse of Meta's reflection in the mirror and she spun around facing Meta. "You didn't tell me that you were not a white girl! Why didn't you tell me you were not a white girl?" Shaken by the director's reaction, yet determined to state her rights, Meta replied, "I was told that the American Girls' Club was financed by Mrs. Whitelaw Reid and other American women for American girl students who came to Paris to study. I felt that I, as an American girl, was entitle to come here."[8] While Miss Acley agreed, she expressed her concern that Meta would not be treated well by the other girls, particularly those from the South. Meta attempted to make the woman understand that she was not concerned about the attitude of the Southern girls. "I haven't come over here to engage in social relations with anyone. I intend to study and get what I can out of my studies and then go back home." While she was awaiting Miss Acley's decision on her stay, Henry Tanner arrived. Upon hearing of Meta's unpleasant reception at the Club, he urged her not to insist on staying and arranged for her to move to a small hotel.

For the first several months of her stay in Paris, Meta studied under Raphael Collin, Augustus Saint-Gaudens, and Antoine Carles, followed by a year at the Academie Colarossi, with lectures on anatomy at the Ecole des Beaux Arts. Resolved not to dwell on her traumatic experience upon her arrival in Paris, she was determined to take advantage of the opportunities that the city offered. She met a young black woman who had come to Paris to study music and the two rented a studio where they lived, worked, and entertained many of their friends from the United States who had come during the Paris Exposition of 1899. As the end of her second year in Paris drew closer, Meta became concerned that her work had not progressed to the extent that she had envisioned. But could she dare to ask for more time, when she had promised to be away from home no longer than two years? She wrote her mother, pleading for one more year in which to master her art. With her mother's consent and financial support, Meta turned her attention to her sculpture.

It was in Paris that Meta met W.E.B. Dubois. Introduced by Thomas Calloway, a frequent visitor to her studio who was in charge of the Negro exhibit at the Paris Exposition of 1900, DuBois invited Meta to be his guest at the banquet at the United States Pavilion at the Exposition to which black visitors were invited.

> Mr. Calloway said he would like to have me come. I said I would be delighted, and asked what the fee would be. Dr. Dubois spoke up then and said, 'There will be no fee. You will come as my guest.' I decided to put on my best bib and tucker, which happened to be my white silk graduation dress and I got it out and pressed it. Dr. Dubois called for me, and I felt proud to have such an escort. He was master of ceremonies, and I sat at his right. From then on, Dr. Dubois and I enjoyed meeting from time to time with other friends visiting Paris.[9]

It was the beginning of a lifelong friendship. Both had similar backgrounds—like Meta, Dubois' mother worked for wealthy white families and his childhood friends were from these families—and both had traveled to Europe to study. Dubois contributed to Meta's knowledge of African and black American politics and his Pan-Africanist philosophy served as the inspiration for two of her works, *Ethiopia Awakening* (1914) and *Mary Turner* (1919). According to DuBois, Meta was one of those persons of ability and genius whom "accidents of education and opportunity had raised on a tidal wave of chance."[10]

During her last year in Paris, Meta was given a letter of introduction to Auguste Rodin, and she went to visit him at his studio in Meudon. In what she recalled as one of the most exciting moments in her life, Rodin met with her and examined several of her models and sketches. He was particularly impressed by an eight-inch plaster sketch of her work entitled *Man Eating His Heart*, inspired by Stephen Crane's poem, "The Heart". He studied the piece for a few moments and then remarked, "my child, you are a sculptor: you have the sense of form in your fingers".[11] At the end of her interview, Rodin agreed to critique her work, adding that he would come to Paris to do so if the sculpture was too large for her to bring to him.

Rodin's endorsement of her work brought with it a recognition of Meta's artistic talent by the Paris art world. Her work was featured in exhibitions, winning awards for its profound portrayal of human suffering. The noted art dealer, Samuel Bing, featured twenty of her works in a one-woman show at his art salon, L'Art Nouveau. Monsieur Bing purchased several pieces from the show. Her art became noted for its themes of horror, pain, and sorrow, thought to be expressions of her feelings of oppression and despair as a black woman, at a time when it was unacceptable for blacks and women to verbalize their opinions about their status in society. With her work selling and receiving high praise from the art critics, it was time for Meta to return to the United States.

After her success in Paris, Meta's return to Philadelphia was a disappointment. She opened a studio, but was unable to sell her work. The United States was not ready to accept a black woman's portrayal of pain and suffering depicted in her sculpture. She found herself unable to earn enough money by selling her art to be financially independent and had to rely on her family for support. When asked why she did not return to Paris, Meta answered that her art was an expression of the American black experience and that she needed to be close to her cultural roots. Her family was also very important to her and she was influenced by their expectations of her, which were consistent with society's image of women at that time: to marry and raise a family, putting career interests aside.

For three years following their first meeting in Westboro, Meta and Solomon continued their relationship. Both had agreed to postpone marriage – he wanted to be in a position to support a wife and to build a house for her and she wanted the opportunity to pursue her career as an artist. In 1907, Meta was commissioned by the Board of the Jamestown Tercentennial Exposition to execute a large sculpture depicting the progress of the African-American since the settlement in Jamestown. She was to be paid fifteen hundred dollars, "...a lot of money in those days. So I went ahead with it."[12] In accepting this commission, she was inspired by the opportunity to demonstrate to the American public her capabilities as an artist and to show the African-American's contribution toward America's progress. The completed work consisted of fifteen tableaux that highlighted the stages in the advancement of the African-American, beginning with the arrival of the first Africans in 1619. The *Negro Tableaux* earned Meta a gold medal and established her reputation as an American artist. Meta would later recall two significant memories of the Exposition, a meeting with President Theodore Roosevelt and another, more sobering experience.

> I didn't know it at the time, but I couldn't eat at any of the restaurants. I became so hungry that, when I visited the exhibit of the Shredded Wheat Company and discovered they were handing out samples, I took some of them. That was all I had to eat during that day of my visit to the Jamestown Exposition.[13]

Dedicated as she was to her sculpture and despite the advice of many of her artist friends in Paris not to marry, Meta still felt that marriage and child-bearing were "part of life". Solomon's salary at the Westboro hospital had been increased to $1800 a year, his promise to build her a house had been fulfilled, and so the couple set a wedding date.

Solomon and Meta were married on February 9, 1909 at St. Thomas Church in Philadelphia. On that afternoon, Meta dressed and came downstairs well ahead of the scheduled time of the wedding and found the church hall deserted. Solomon had insisted that the ceremony begin at six o'clock and was known to be punctual.

> I wore a *crepe de chine* dress, a veil that one of my cousins had loaned me – a voluminous tulle veil. I wondered where everybody was until I noticed my prospective husband standing there and waiting for me without uttering a word. He wasn't supposed to see me until the proper time, but there he was! Suddenly the six o'clock whistle blew. I said, 'I thought we were supposed to be married at six o'clock.' He explained there was some mix-up about the carriages and that's what delayed everyone. So I wasn't married at six, even though I had four ministers there to do the trick.[14]

The ceremony was indeed performed by four ministers: the Rev. Mr. Townsend, rector of the Episcopal Church in Atlantic City; the Rev. Mr. Deaver, rector of the Colored Episcopal Church in Atlantic City; Father Alexander Cartier, rector of St. Thomas Church in Philadelphia, and the Rev. Mr. E.G. Knight, an old friend. Fred Hemings, who was reported to be a descendant of Sally Hemings, was Fuller's best man. Following the ceremony, a wedding reception was provided by Margaret Brown, the former housekeeper of Meta's grandmother, who had died earlier that winter. The Fullers then left for their new home in Framingham, stopping in Brooklyn, New York where they were entertained by Solomon's cousins, the Jarratts.

Chapter Seven

Pioneer in American Psychiatry
Framingham
1909

As a black professional in America it is sometimes so difficult to find true acceptance in either the black or the white communities that I often feel like an outsider to both. Alienation seems to be the price of living with a foot in each world.

Lawrence Otis Graham, *Member of the Club: Reflections on Life in a Racially Polarized World*[1]

Solomon Fuller had been determined to build a home for his new wife that he could take her to after their wedding. His friend, John Merriam, who was a trustee of Westboro Insane Hospital, lived in the nearby town of Framingham and suggested to Fuller that he build his house there. Situated twenty miles west of Boston, which was accessible by train, it seemed an ideal location for the Fullers to settle, and Solomon bought a lot on Warren Road in a residential section of the town. The largest industry in the growing urban community was the manufacture of wagon wheels, with a workforce made up of large numbers of Irish, Italian and French immigrants. At that time, African Americans accounted for a very small percentage of the population of Framingham. With the exception of the blackface minstrel shows held at the Elmwood Opera House and the Gorman Theatre, blacks were for the most part, invisible.[2] It wasn't until the Fullers began construction on their home that the residents of the affluent white neighborhood learned that their new neighbors were black.

Despite the fact that the house that the Fullers were building was more expensive than others in the neighborhood, a petition was circulated by their neighbors, led by a prominent businessman who lived next door to the property, to keep out the respected physician and the well-known artist. A committee was formed that was authorized to make an offer to buy the couple out. John Merriam offered them another piece of property on Union Avenue, Framingham's main street, but Solomon and Meta refused his offer. When the house was completed, Meta recalled, 'It was the most distinctive-looking house on the street, and more artistic than any of the others!"[3]

> No sooner did we move in here than I used to go up and down the street, never looking right nor left," recalled Meta. "Little by little, the people on the block began to come over to ask favors, to borrow something – you know, sugar or eggs or potatoes. One of our neighbors, a man named Arthur Bent, who had met Doctor on the street while we were building, said then that he thought it was a dastardly thing that these people were doing in trying to keep us out, and that, when we came here to live, he would bring his wife to call on us, which he did. That sort of tided the whole thing over – when people saw what Arthur Bent was doing, and what a few others were beginning to do. The lady next door called herself Auntie Brown to the children. She and her husband had been among the ringleaders to sign the petition to keep us out."[4]

Following his wedding and the move to his new home, Solomon Fuller returned to his research and teaching, focusing his attention on the organic basis for dementia, schizophrenia (then called dementia praecox), and manic-depressive psychosis. Inspired by his work with Alzheimer and Kraepelin, he developed techniques for the study of brain tissue, while at the same time, studying the behavioral manifestations of patients. Fuller was interested in those psychological disorders that appeared to have no organic cause and he began to explore functional psychological conditions and the effects that the new psychotherapy being pioneered by Sigmund Freud and others might have on those disorders. Since the turn of the century, New England had become the center of American psychiatry, influenced by an emphasis on social reform and the recognition of scientific psychology as an academic discipline.[5] Fuller's established reputation as neuropathologist, at a time when mental illness was considered a disease of the brain, and his experience in Germany, which gave him a proficiency in German and knowledge of psychiatry, set him apart from his American contemporaries.

By 1909, Clark University in Worcester, Massachusetts, under the direction of G. Stanley Hall, had become the center for the development of new ideas and approaches in the psychodynamic and psychoanalytic models of psychiatry in the United States. Hall, an academic psychologist, had established a graduate program in psychology in partnership with Worcester State Hospital and recruited such leaders in the field as Adolf Meyer. Like Fuller, he had also traveled to Germany for postgraduate education. In speaking of his conversations with Dr. Hall, Fuller described him as being "...one of the most brilliant minds I've met – photographic and encyclopedic memory. The librarian said he read two laundry baskets of books a day."[6] Fuller later became Hall's personal physician and for years they continued their friendship and mutual respect, despite the charge by many blacks that Hall's publications supported the racist assumption that blacks were inferior to whites.

Fuller was one of the first exponents of the new psychoanalytic theories. Like many other American physicians who had backgrounds in neurology, he was looking to the new insights of Sigmund Freud for additional understanding of nervous disorders. Professor Hodge, a biology professor at Clark, was impressed by Fuller's autopsy material and invited him to lecture at the university. The faculty had worked only with animals and they wanted Fuller to integrate his human pathological and histological material into their courses. But..."having little time and much intrepidation, I gave only one lecture at Clark."[7]

In 1909, Fuller was among a group of psychologists who were invited to attend the Clark Celebration, the 20th anniversary of the opening of Clark University. His presentation was entitled "Cerebral Histology, with Special Reference to Histopathology of the Psychoses". This event also marked Sigmund Freud's first visit to the United States. He arrived in New York in late August of 1909, at the invitation of G. Stanley Hall, to give a series of lectures. He was accompanied by Carl Jung from Zurich and Sandor Ferenczi from Budapest. During the centennial celebration, he delivered a lecture and received an honorary degree from the university.

> The most important event of our Worcester visit was an address given by Sigmund Freud on the twentieth anniversary of Clark University. I was deeply impressed by the lucidity of his mind and the simplicity of his delivery. Among the array of professors, looking stiff and important in their university caps and gowns, Sigmund Freud, in ordinary attire, unassuming, almost shrinking, stood out like a giant among pygmies. He had aged somewhat since I had heard him in Vienna in 1896. He had been reviled then as a Jew and irresponsible innovator; now he was a world figure; but neither obloquy nor fame had influenced the great man.[8]
>
> Emma Goldman

Freud was very pleased by the reception that he received at the Clark Celebration.

> In Europe I felt as though I was despised, but in America I found myself received by the foremost men as an equal. As I stepped on the platform at Worcester to deliver my five lectures on psychoanalysis, it seemed like the realization of some incredible daydream. Psychoanalysis was no longer a product of delusion; it had become a valuable part of reality.[9]
>
> Sigmund Freud

The Clark University lectures and Freud's visit marked a turning point in the practice of American psychiatry. Psychoanalytic theory had spread throughout Europe and now to the United States, becoming a major influence in psychiatric teaching and practice. For the first time, it was understood that there was some explanation to the peculiar variations of behavior seen in the psychiatric patient. Freud's theory was based on the premise that hysterical symptoms were the result of past events that had been forgotten by the conscious mind, but had been retained in the unconscious mind. Treatment of these symptoms involved the uncovering of these past events through psychoanalysis, a process in which the patient's dreams, memories, and thoughts were examined. Reconstruction of the history of the patient and the patient's symptoms was accomplished through methodical observation and questioning. Like Fuller, Freud's background was in neurology and histopathology.

Fuller continued to exchange theories with several of the leading psychiatrists of that era who he had met at the Clark symposium, including Carl Jung, Alfred Adler, and Adolf Meyer.

> I have never gone around with anyone who in anyway approached Kraepelin, except perhaps Adolph Meyer. Adolph Meyer is not so clear in explaining his ideas as is Kraepelin. If you talked with Adolph Meyer and saw cases with him, you were impressed with his knowledge, but if you read one of his papers, he seems involved in his thinking. I never got very much out of reading Adolph Meyer or listening to his papers because he knows so much about the thing and he pulls in so many things from all various directions, beclouds the issue apparently. But talking to him and seeing him and working the patients is different.[10]

Several years later, Meyer recommended Fuller for a position at Johns Hopkins. His application was rejected because he was a "colored man".[11] It was also during this period that Fuller developed friendships with Henry Mills Hurd at Johns Hopkins and Edward Brush, a good friend who encouraged the publication of his papers in the *American Journal of Insanity*.

As psychiatry became more closely identified as a field of medicine, psychiatrists began to redefine their role with a new emphasis on scientific research and care outside of the psychiatric hospital. Psychiatrists who incorporated Freudian concepts into their practice had little contact with public mental hospitals, treating their patients in smaller private hospitals and in private practice. With the shift in the focus of treatment of mental illness from mental hospitals to community care, physicians began to look into the social aspects of mental disease and its relationship to conditions in society.

Massachusetts had been the first state to accept voluntary patients into its mental hospitals.[12] In the past, admission had been arranged through requests from a poor-officer or a relative. Most of the voluntary patients who were admitted to Westboro Insane Hospital were considered to be curable to the extent that they could return to the community following treatment. At the suggestion of the State Board of Insanity, a therapeutic colony had been established in 1902, a mile from the main hospital, to accommodate 100 male patients. A year later, a second colony was opened for women patients about half a mile from the hospital. In 1907, a farm colony for men was set up that allowed the patients to experience a normal farm life. The admission of voluntary patients, along with the changes that were occurring in the treatment of mental illness, led the Westboro Insane Hospital to change its name to Westborough State Hospital in 1909 and to create a therapeutic community on hospital grounds.[13]

While he continued his research at Westborough State Hospital and his teaching at Boston University, Fuller took on additional duties as a visiting neurologist at Massachusetts Memorial Hospital, Framingham's Marlboro Hospital, and Pennsylvania's Allentown State Hospital. His appointment at Allentown was made possible through the efforts of his old friend, Dr. Henry Klopp, who became the hospital's superintendent. Concurrent with his duties as pathologist at Westborough, Fuller served as the director of the Clinical Society Commission of Massachusetts. His son, Solomon Jr., recalled that his father was often asked to work with Dr. Harvey Cushing as a consulting pathologist. Dr. Cushing, the Chief of Surgery at Peter Brent Brigham Hospital in Boston, was a pioneer in the field of neurosurgery.

> Cushing invited him to watch an operation. So they were all in their masks and standing around. Harvey started to go in on the patient's left side of his brain and Dad flinched. He couldn't say it with all those people around, but he gathered his courage and whispered to Cushing, "If it were me, I would go in on the other side." "Well, I suppose so," Cushing replied. And he went in on the other side. And Dad had been right.[14]

Fuller was invited to give several lectures at Harvard, where he also took courses in psychology and spiritualism with William James. He began to practice psychiatry, integrating the new psychology in the treatment of such mental disorders as schizophrenia and manic depression. While Fuller never fully accepted the method of psychoanalysis, he recognized the importance of its dynamic concepts and viewed it as a tool which could be refined for understanding behavior and emotional disturbances. He identified with the principles of Adolf Meyer, which emphasized the importance of treating the patient as an individual, taking into consideration the patient's history and social situation in addition to his/her complaints or symptoms.

Fuller's orientation in his practice of psychiatry was the same as the one that he had learned in the laboratory – careful observation and scientific reasoning.

> A typical workday began around 9:30 in the morning and lasted until after midnight. Mornings were spent at the Westborough Hospital and afternoons, teaching at Boston University. Following his return from Boston in the late afternoon, Fuller would see patients in his home into the late evening. An avid collector of books, he would often read until two o'clock in the morning[15]

With the birth of Solomon and Meta's first child, Solomon Carter Jr., on March 10, 1910, Meta retired from the art world to devote time to her family. Prior to her move to Framingham, she had stored her art pieces in a Philadelphia warehouse to be sent to Framingham upon the completion of her new home. Each month she would resolve to return to Philadelphia and pack them for shipping, but with a house to maintain and a new baby, she was never able to make the trip. Her aunt was instructed to send the boxes to Framingham, but before they could be shipped, the warehouse was destroyed by fire. Most of Meta's sculptures and sketches over the last 16 years, including her famous piece, *Man Eating His Heart*, and other works created in Paris, were lost. Only *The Wretched* and a few others survived the fire.[16] Pressured by her husband that her primary responsibility was to raise a family and manage a household, Meta put aside her dream to become an international artist.

Chapter Eight

Contributions to Science and Medicine
Westborough
1911

A man standing against the current, holding his own.

Solomon Carter Fuller, Jr.[1]

Solomon Carter Fuller's professional life of scientific research, teaching and clinical practice led him to become well respected in the field of neurology. His profession gave him legitimacy and prestige in a society which continued to view blacks as second class citizens. While racial oppression and segregation was widespread and taken for granted in the south, Fuller was not spared the effects of racism in the north. Although Fuller enjoyed a certain amount of social privilege, he was still subjected to racial prejudice.

> I was finishing some work on senile plaques and there was some literature down at the Harvard Medical School Pathological Laboratory that I wanted to consult. I couldn't find it in the Boston Medical Library and I wrote Dr. Councilman to see if I could have access to certain volumes he had in his collection. He wrote me back he would be very glad to give me access to them and to come down on a certain date and he would be glad to make them accessible for me so I went down on the particular date. Now this shows the difference in men (as compared to Ehrlich). I was to be there at 9 A.M. He wasn't there – he hadn't come in yet. 10 or 15 minutes later he came in and he looked at me, you know, as if to say "what do you want" and I told him who I was – I had written him about consulting certain volumes – he said, "oh yes, yes", and called the deiner – that is the ordinary servant around there in the

laboratory and he said, you take the Doctor and see that he has access to certain volumes in the room of the main laboratory there. So I went in there and got the material and I did not see him after that. And when I came out to say goodbye to him and to thank him, he wasn't anywhere around. And I had been in there because it was something (material) that wasn't (allowed) going out, I had copied it and I had been in there an hour in all and that was all the attention I got from Councilman.

Well, he was one of those old Southern gentlemen – he came from Kentucky you know, and he was astounded, that is what it seemed to me, that a colored person had come down there and wanted a scientific relationship with him. He showed – now I may be wrong, this old fellow is dead now and I may have been oversensitive and misinterpreted his actions – but it is so striking in contrast from the reception I got from the leading medical men in the world at that time, you know. I knew very well you couldn't go into any American university as I did up there in Frankfurt. You certainly couldn't. You couldn't get near them. And that was his attitude.[2]

In the years following his return from Germany, Fuller continued his work in the pathology laboratory at Westborough. The reputation of the laboratory had grown and it was now one of the two laboratories in Massachusetts that did the analyses for the Wasserman tests for syphilis for the state hospitals. The laboratory also became known as a highly regarded training site for medical students who were interested in neuropathology.

...when people came up to the Harvard Medical School and wanted courses in neuropathology you know, and they had been working in general pathology – Southard then was the head of this thing. He was the head neuropathologist as well as the neuropathologist of the Harvard Medical School. If you went to Mallory (the ranking general pathologist in the U.S.) he would send them out to me. Dr. Southard had a summer course in neuropathology – sent the entire class to Westboro for certain parts of the course.

Belding (later professor of pathology and bacteriologist at B.U., pathologist of Mass. Game Commission), after he had been a pupil of mine, went over to Harvard, got a Harvard degree, did a lot of work over there and used to go over to Mallory a great deal – it was just across the street - so he got to the point where he wanted to brush up on the neuropathology and he wanted to go and work with Southard...So Mallory said, 'Why do you want to go with Southard?' 'Well he is professor of neuropathology there and has the best facilities and I thought it would be a good place to go' and Mallory said to him, 'If you want to go into pathology and you are interested in histopathology of cerebral cortex , you go up to Westboro.[3]

Fuller regularly published papers on his research in neuropathology and clinical neurology. His work with Alzheimer, which had demonstrated the organic nature of general paresis and established the histological characteristics, inspired Fuller to continue his research on the symptomatology and pathology of what was now known as Alzheimer's disease. In 1907, he reported on a large group of demented cases (paralytics, senile dementias, alcoholics, syphilitics, and persons with abnormally small skulls) he had autopsied at Westborough.[4] His findings were based on his analysis of microscopic slides of brain sections and patient records to determine the unique histopathology ascribed to Alzheimer's presenile dementia. His article, illustrated with seventeen microphotographs, reported his findings of plaques and globular structures (to be designated amyloid) and various stages of degenerating neurofibrils not constrained to the senile sections.

> He (Alzheimer) presented these group cases shortly after I left (Germany), for a meeting of the Southwest German Psychiatric Society, something like our New England Society, and I began to look over some of my material and I found a case. Then I began to study and looking after these plaques and things of that sort and got the first thing published in the English language of Alzheimer's disease. I watched the literature pretty carefully. There were some cases published in English, but they were not recognized as such. One by a man named Betts up in Buffalo.
>
> He had included it in some other thing but he had missed the characteristic thing altogether, just as I had missed it in the first case of mine and I began to assemble all the cases and had one to report. Then I came across two others, one of which was reported by Dr. Clarke and then I collected all the cases which had been published up to that time, there were 11. That is the first publication concerning Alzheimer's in the English language.[5]

Alzheimer's disease was not universally accepted as a new dementia classification. In the 1910 edition of his widely accepted psychiatric text, Kraepelin had created the new disease entity renaming senile dementia as two distinct diseases, presenile and senile dementia, subtitling presenile dementia as "Morbus Alzheimer".[6] Yet, the characteristic plaques had been described by the Hungarian Blocq as early as 1892 and more completely by Fischer in 1907. Adding to the debate was an article written by Alzheimer in 1911, in which he made an attempt to clarify the situation by a review of the contemporary literature. He concluded by questioning whether the cases that were being identified by his name should be separated from the senile dementias.[7]

Fuller's doubts about Alzheimer's disease representing a true entity as suggested by Kraepelin became evident in his later writings. In a study of miliary plaques and neurofibrils found in the brains of elderly patients at Westborough, with and without psychoses, he compared these cases with the brains of young subjects who had been diagnosed with various mental diseases.

> I wanted some material from Mallory and was then working on senile plaques and I went down to Mallory (Boston City Hospital) to get some material from the old seniles who had died down there without psychosis.
>
> And I took in with me some of the things (slides, photography, etc.). I inquired for Mallory. He received me in a reserved sort of manner but not – it was friendly – but in a dignified manner – I showed him things I had been doing and why I wanted the so called normal senile material to see if there was

any difference in it from the senile material with psychosis. He was very cooperative – he gave me, I think, 6 cases and I always came in when I had anything I wanted him to look at. I would always take it in to him. He would examine it with interest and make suggestions – oftentimes he would make no suggestions – when he probably thought it was alright.[8]

In 1911, Fuller published another article on Alzheimer's disease. Once again, he was puzzled over the literary race to report prematurely on a syndrome which seemed to have a variable composition in the minds of different observers. Many of the cases he reported had, in addition to plaques in a variety of states of degeneration, glial proliferation and necrosis and combinations of brain atrophy, neurofibril and vascular changes exclusive of their classified confines. In his article, he questioned the significance of plaques and neurofibrillar changes as pathognomic of Alzheimer's disease and he suggested that arteriosclerosis may not be the cause of the disease as some had thought.[9]

Fuller examined the pathology of 92 selected brains that most fit the criteria developed by his former European colleagues and found one that measured up to Alzheimer's standard. In 1912, he published this case, along with the first comprehensive clinical review of the pathology and histories of all Alzheimer's cases that had been reported up to that time – a total of 79 cases.[10,11] His exceptional photographs showed the extensive degeneration and plaques and tangles that were becoming known as characteristic clinical findings in patients with Alzheimer's disease. In this article, Fuller continued to refer to the plaques in Alzheimer's disease as Fischer's plaques and mentioned the inconsistencies of strict criteria, pointing out that the important variations in the mental symptoms and microscopic descriptions were represented by too few cases to justify anything comparable to the paradigm.

As he continued his research, Fuller became more the critical commentator, publishing a third article to illustrate the inconsistencies in the published reports of others, including Alzheimer.

> Their clinical histories and anatomical findings best comport with the severe forms of senile dementia. If, then, these are cases of atypical senile dementia, the question could fittingly arise why a special clinical designation – 'Alzheimer's disease' – since, after all, they are but part of a general disorder.
>
> Still, the profession must remain indebted to Alzheimer for having first called attention to this type of case. He himself did not claim a distinct clinical entity for the group…for there was no good ground for supposing a special pathognomonic process; that the cases were representative of a senile psychosis-atypical senile dementia, a view which is shared by Lafora (1911), Jansen (1912) and other writers.[12]

With the arrival of the Fullers' second son, William Thomas on June 9, 1911, Meta devoted her time to caring for her family. But, a letter arrived in 1912 that would inspire her to take up her art again. The letter came from W.E.B. DuBois, her old friend from her years in Paris. DuBois had founded the

National Association for the Advancement of Colored People (NAACP) in 1910, an organization to promote civil and political liberty for blacks, and was now in New York, editing the organization's newspaper, *Crisis*. Remembering her portrayal of the suffering of black people through her art, DuBois asked Meta to make a colossal figure of the Spirit of Emancipation to celebrate the fiftieth anniversary of the Emancipation Proclamation in New York. A pageant, written by DuBois, was to be presented at one of the city's armories and African American painting, sculpture and handicrafts were to be on exhibit. Meta's sculpture would be used to express the meaning of emancipation. DuBois' request revived the artist's creative spirit. She bought new tools and set up a studio in the attic of her home, where she created a statue of emancipation that depicted an African American boy and girl, standing under an overshadowing figure representing their servitude. They have just been set free and behind them, humanity is urging them to go forward, while racial hatred is holding them back. Confused, they stand looking to the future. Following the exhibition, the seven-foot plaster statue was stored in the Fuller's garage and forgotten until 1999, when a bronze casting of the sculpture was unveiled in Harriet Tubman Square Park, located in Boston's South End.

Meta continued to work in her small studio whenever time would allow. Her work turned mostly to portraits and traditional religious themes. Religion had always been an important and socially acceptable method of expression for blacks in America since the days of slavery when they were not allowed to meet in public groups. Religion also provided individual solace when hopes for changing the future for blacks were bleak. Velma Hoover, a friend of Meta Fuller, later wrote, "I believe that the direction which Mrs. Fuller's work took reflected the effects of her resignation of her life of 'retirement' into conventional marriage and family life."[13]

In 1914, Fuller developed and edited the *Westborough State Hospital Papers*, a journal reporting the medical research of hospital staff. The hospital had begun expanding its services to the community. Arrangements were made to board patients in the community and out-patient clinics were established, accomplishing the goals set forth twenty-six years earlier by the Westborough Hospital report of 1888.[14] Up to this time, private psychiatric practice was rare, with most psychiatrists working in state mental hospitals. In the shift from institutional organic psychiatry to community-based psychoanalytically oriented practitioners, the psychoanalytic movement grew and began to have an influence on medical education and practice. Contributing to this transformation was the establishment of professional organizations that were focused on the study and application of the methods developed by Freud.

Previously viewed negatively by the American medical profession, psychiatry was becoming a recognized specialty as evidenced by the merging of the boards of psychiatry and neurology in the mid-1900's. The rapid growth of private practice in psychiatry, along with the social and political developments in Europe, brought psychoanalytically oriented European psychiatrists to the United States to study – the reverse of previous years. The once highly respected institutions of learning that had inspired Fuller to travel to Germany were now crippled by the outbreak of World War I.

Fuller transcended science into practice, establishing himself as America's first black psychiatrist in 1919. The number of black physicians in the United States remained small, continuing to be affected by limited opportunities for blacks to attain access to medical education and training.[15] Fuller practiced psychiatry with psychotherapy, following the work of Freud, Jung and Adler. Interested in psychological problems that appeared to have no organic cause, he spent much time studying psychoanalytic theory and methods.

> My brothers and I used to go to the pond and catch frogs. One day, Dad asked me to get him a frog, which I did. Several weeks later, I asked him what became of the frog. Dad said 'I had a patient and she would come to me once every month complaining that she had a frog in her stomach.
>
> After several months of unsuccessful therapy to eliminate her obsession, I made an appointment with this woman, induced vomiting and seriptiously [sic] tossed the frog in the vomit to convince her that she was now rid of the frog in her stomach. She never again complained about a frog in her stomach.'[16]

For many years, Fuller maintained an office in Boston and in his home. His practice drew patients from Boston, Framingham and Westborough, who were treated regardless of their color or ability to pay.

The state of race relations in the United States had deteriorated in the years between 1915 and 1920. Increased feelings of confidence and higher aspirations among blacks created fear in many white Americans, setting the stage for the rebirth of the Ku Klux Klan in 1915. The revival of the Klan spread beyond the southern states, as evidenced by the bombing of St. Stephen's Church in Framingham in 1916. Burning crosses appeared in the Fullers' community and on August 10, 1920, a large group of townspeople staged a confrontation with members of the Klan. Shots were fired and 75 Klansmen were arrested.[17]

Black soldiers had experienced certain privileges and opportunities while serving in the military that were denied to them at home. Their high expectations coupled with the frustrations of the African American population challenged the existing order of American society. This challenge was met by a demonstration of brute force, known as "putting the Negro back in his place." Many blacks were lynched during and after the war. The summer of 1919 became known as the "Red Summer", with more than 70 lynchings, 10 of them blacks still in uniform. Twenty-six race riots broke out in the first postwar year, fueled by racial hatred compounded by the economic recession.[18]

During the First World War, Fuller was a member of Advisory Board No. 17, Boston Society for Psychiatry and Neurology. A Division of Neurology and Psychiatry had been established in the office of the Surgeon General in response to the identification of large numbers of soldiers diagnosed with neuropsychiatric disabilities. A plan for the diagnosis and treatment of these individuals was developed, necessitating the mobilization and training of civilian mental health professionals. In order to do his part in making the world safe for democracy, Fuller offered his services as a neuropsychiatrist to the military. A letter from the War Department dated August 1, 1918, written in response to his request to serve in the war effort, made the case that his race would be an obstacle in attaining military rank:

My dear Dr. Fuller:

The need for your services continues. On the other hand, there are some obstacles in the way of obtaining your services. I find that it would not be possible to grant you a commission until you have been naturalized.

Under a law recently passed, one who is not now a citizen can be immediately naturalized upon enlisting in the Army. We are utilizing this law in obtaining commissions for a number of men. The process is for the man to enlist in the Army as a private. We usually have him do this here in Washington, in order that, as soon as he is enlisted, we can order him to St. Elizabeth's Hospital, where the situation is understood. The man is then given a ten day leave of absence. During these ten days his naturalization is completed and his application for a commission put through. By the time it is necessary for him to report back to duty, he usually has his commission, and goes out as an officer. We have recently succeeded in doing this in two cases.

The other obstacle is unfortunately in regard to race. I am sure you wish me to speak frankly on this matter, as you know my own personal feelings. It is not likely that a commission higher than that of lieutenant could be granted to you on the start. It is possible that you might obtain a captaincy, but this is doubtful. It is not likely that it would ever be possible for you to obtain a commission higher than that of captain.

This might handicap you somewhat in your work in the Army, but I think not seriously. If, under these conditions, you feel that you can apply, you may be sure that you will be most cordially welcomed by this division.

Your services are needed, and you would receive every support from us.

Sincerely,
Frankwood E. Williams, Major, M.R.C.
Office of the Surgeon General,
War Department,
Washington, D.C.[19]

Fuller's reply, dated August 5, 1918:

My dear Dr. Williams:

The very frank tone of your letter of August 1, is greatly appreciated. The method for overcoming the first obstacle which you mentioned, namely by enlisting as a private and under the new law attaining citizenship within a short period is satisfactory. This I would gladly undertake.

The other obstacle, however, is something more than an obstacle, as ordinarily understood; apparently it is an impasse infranchissable [sic] The conditions laid down with this latter obstacle seem to preclude the possibility of rendering the sort of service for which by training and experience, I am best qualified. Needless to add my regrets, but in the face of the clearly defined limitations imposed for me, I believe the work could be more effectively performed by one with fewer handicaps.

You will understand, I am sure, that to serve effectively the group of men in the army with whom I would be identified, would be the greatest possible satisfaction, but if I cannot serve them effectively – and I do not see how this can be done under "the conditions" – the only course open to me with respect to your offer must be obvious. I feel, therefore, that in my present position as pathologist and director of clinical psychiatry, in an established institution administering to the public need, the opportunity for service of a worth while character is greater than in the very restricted field which your letter outlines.

Believe me.

Very sincerely yours,
Dr. Solomon Carter Fuller[20]

Solomon and Meta's third son, Perry James, was born in 1916. In addition to the responsibilities of caring for three small children, Meta managed to find time to continue her sculpture. In 1915, she had received a second prize award by the Women's Peace Party for her work, *Peace Halting the Ruthlessness of War*. Considered among her most outstanding works, the sculpture depicts a blind soldier on a blind horse plowing through a mass of humanity. As her children grew, Meta worked on her sculpture while they were in school and at night. After the children were in bed, the couple would typically spend the evening sitting on the living room sofa facing the fireplace. While Solomon sat reading, Meta would often work on her sculpture, one of which was a portrait bust of her husband. Although Fuller felt that his wife's first obligation was to her family, he enjoyed her art and helped her with exhibitions.

> Doctor felt that my first duty was to the family, the children. He said I spent too much time outside. But he enjoyed my work. He would give me constructive criticism. He entertained the people who would come to see my work.[21]

The Fuller's home became a gathering place for many of their friends, black and white, artists and intellectuals. One frequent visitor was Meta's close friend, W.E.B. DuBois, the black sociologist. They had maintained contact in the years following their first meeting in Paris and shared the experience of rejection they encountered from American society. DuBois was known for his writings about the poor social conditions of blacks in the United States, the same conditions illustrated by Meta in her art. Solomon, Jr. recalled a comment made by DuBois while visiting the Fuller home:

> I can remember hearing Dr. Dubois say, 'I don't think we're going to hear very much from American Negroes until first we hear a lot more about crime in America.' I was 10 years old at the time and too young to understand what that meant. But I remembered it until the time came when I could understand it and I thought, 'How amazing!' In other words, there is always the element of criminology in a group's advancement. It was not a popular notion, therefore it hasn't been publicized much.[22]

Other visitors to the Fuller home included Paul Robeson, the black actor and singer; Harry Burleigh, known for his role in popularizing Negro spirituals; and Roland Hayes, the famous tenor who would stay at their house whenever he sang with the Boston Symphony. Solomon, Jr. remembers that "all the great blacks came to our house because they weren't welcome in public areas. Now, in those days, we knew that we couldn't go into a restaurant in Framingham." Many of the visiting intellectuals were so achievement-oriented that they would always ask the Fullers' sons, "How are your marks in school?" and "Where are you going to college?"

Journalists who came to Fuller's home seeking an interview were not welcomed, according to Solomon, Jr. "Dad didn't want to talk to writers because he didn't want to become known as a 'colored psychiatrist'." When it was suggested that he should make his professional accomplishments known, he would reply, "My work will tell that in the end."

> ....Our parents had a wonderfully close domestic life. Mother kept on with her sculpting and eventually had a studio located about a quarter of a mile from our house, where she worked and taught. Besides that, she was a cofounder of the Framingham Dramatic Club and was active in church affairs – she was a pioneer in creating religious dramas – and in the women's suffrage movement. But my parents each respected the other's career and interests. They did not have disagreements in front of us children and concealed from us their grief over the racism they encountered.
>
> Like many people of their generation, both Mother and Dad were rather formal. For example, we took all our meals in the dining room and always dressed properly for them. I learned my grammar around the table. When you made a verbal lapse, you were corrected – gently – almost before the words came out of your mouth. I only wish more young people today had the benefit of the kind of upbringing I received. Both my parents were busy people, but they always seemed to have enough time to give me and my brothers loving attention.[23]

Despite his busy schedule, Fuller found time for his neighbors. They often came to the house seeking medical advice and shots for allergies. He would regularly go down in the woods near his home to visit an old black man who couldn't read and who, according to Fuller's son, "used the most eloquent profanity you've ever heard. My father could find substance in people that others wouldn't even look at."[24]

Harold Fay, the son of a local minister and a neighbor of the Fullers, was also a frequent visitor to the Fuller home. His son, Solomon, remembered, "He would come to the house, with his hair disheveled and with a station wagon full of dogs."[25] Fuller took an interest in the young man's research on the transmission of sounds under water and would spend time rowing Fay around a nearby lake so that he could conduct his investigations. Fay later established the Submarine Signal Company in Boston, which developed the concept of sonar signals. When he was unsuccessful in his attempt to interest the U.S. military in his ideas, he enlisted Fuller's help in creating public awareness of his project. Fuller borrowed a colleague's boat that was docked at the Yacht Club in Newport, Rhode Island, and the two took the boat at night into the Newport harbor, generating enough mysterious sounds to disturb the sleep of the city's wealthy population. The incident resulted in a newspaper story, which generated interest by the military in the use of sonar. Fay's innovations in underwater signaling led to the development of submarine detectors in World War I, which were used by both the Americans and the British.[26]

In 1919, Fuller resigned from Westborough State Hospital, transferring his research activities to Boston. The hospital's board voted to allow him to remain on staff on a part-time basis. He continued his clinical instruction in the Department of Neurology and Psychiatry at Boston University's School of Medicine, while also maintaining his position as a consulting neurologist at Massachusetts Memorial Hospital. The war had ended and many of the hospital's medical staff who had enlisted were now returning to their posts.

More than 400,000 blacks also served in the United States Armed Forces during the First World War. Facilities providing adequate care and treatment to blacks were limited and unavailable in many areas of the country, particularly in the south where there were few hospital accommodations for blacks and the segregated colored wards were poorly equipped and in disrepair. Following the end of the war, the United States Veterans Bureau began building hospitals for disabled soldiers. Black veterans who had fought alongside white soldiers found themselves excluded from admission to many of these facilities. Faced with increasing pressure from black veterans, their families and the black community, the Harding Administration agreed to develop a plan to meet the health care needs of the disabled black veteran. Since the majority of the blacks who served in the war were from the south, the decision was made to build a hospital specifically designated for their care in Tuskegee, Alabama.[27] In collaboration with the Tuskegee Institute, the Veterans Bureau began construction of a 600-bed hospital in 1921. Originally named the "Hospital for Sick and Injured Colored War Veterans", the facility was designed to treat primarily neuropsychiatric patients and patients with tuberculosis.

The hospital opened under the direction of a white superintendent, Colonel Robert C. Stanley, who staffed the hospital with white doctors and nurses. Black nursemaids were hired to prevent contact between the white staff and black patients. Infuriated by the racist policies in a facility designated to treat black patients, the National Medical Association, a professional organization representing black physicians, joined with the National Association for the Advancement of Colored People (NAACP) and successfully lobbied to replace the white medical staff with a black staff. To staff the hospital with qualified black physicians, the National Medical Association was requested to submit a list of candidates from its membership within sixty days. The sixty-day limit for recruitment of black staff seemed a difficult task to accomplish due to the small number of trained and experienced black physicians in the country. The effects of America's racial climate were being felt in the country's medical schools and hospitals. Most white medical schools in the south and many in the north continued to refuse to admit black students. Because of the small number of accredited hospitals that would accept black trainees, the opportunities for internships and residencies for black medical school graduates were limited. Denied access to hospitals, clinics, and professional associations, black physicians found it difficult to practice medicine and encountered more difficulties in moving up the medical hierarchy than did white physicians.

> About this time the Veteran's Hospital in Tuskegee was to be opened. I had been in correspondence with General Hines of the Veterans' Administration with respect to my taking over the organization of the Mental Department of the Institution, which, at the time I did not feel I could undertake for various reasons. There were two requests from the Veterans' Administration and the third which asked that, since I could not myself undertake the work, to select some promising young men and provide some clinical training in Psychiatry. This I was glad to do. I believed then and it has so proven this would be valuable experience.[28]

Fuller agreed to train a small group of recent black medical school graduates in neuropsychiatry. For their psychiatric training, he made arrangements for them to study under Dr. John P. Sutherland, professor of anatomy at Boston University School of Medicine, and to work as volunteer interns under the direction of Dr. Macfie Campbell at the Psychiatric Hospital in Boston. In November, 1923, five black physicians (Drs. Toussaint T. Tildon, George Branche, Simon Johnson, Harvey Davis, and Drue King) completed the training and reported for duty in the hospital's neuropsychiatric service. One of the group, Dr. Tildon, became the clinical director and later, hospital director. Another, Dr. Branche, supervised the activities of the hospital's mental services. These men went on to train other young black physicians in psychiatry. Fuller's teaching on syphilis also enabled them to diagnose black veterans who had been previously misdiagnosed as having behavioral disorders and had been discharged from the military due to bad conduct, making them ineligible for veterans' benefits.[29]

By 1929, The Tuskegee Veterans Hospital staff had achieved national recognition.

> I am told that this hospital has been rated since it was first established as one of the best managed veterans hospitals in the country, both as to administration and in the character of scientific work done.
> Dr. Louis T. Wright, *The Crisis*[30]

Other leading figures in medicine who studied under Fuller included Winfred Overholser, a graduate of Boston University School of Medicine in 1916, who was Commissioner of Mental Health in Massachusetts, later appointed by President Roosevelt as superintendent of St. Elizabeth's Psychiatric Hospital in Washington, D.C. and served as President of the

American Psychiatric Association; and Karl Menninger, a founder of the Menninger Clinic, who, while a student at Harvard Medical School, sat in on a lecture of Dr. Fuller's, entitled "Window of the Soul (The Eye)". In a letter written to Thomas Webster in 1977, Menninger says of Fuller: "I remember his teaching in the Harvard Medical Program. I can still see Doctor Fuller and hear his gentle, kindly voice, and remember his deliberate and courteous manner."[31]

Chapter Nine

The Later Years
Framingham
1933

All the individuals quoted so far have one thing in common: they are all people who have crashed through the "big gate" from the Negro world into the larger white world beyond. There is a certain suggestion in this that the further a person has moved across that threshold, the further he is likely to be from Africa in almost every way. His early encounters were either less sensitively experienced or, more likely, with latter day success, are less sensitively remembered. He is, in any case, less concerned with any African ingredient in his background or individual makeup. He is a man who has established his individuality not only as a "Negro" but as a particular person whose gifts have wrung recognition from society at large. To this extent he has "solved" (if that is the word") the problem of his own individual identity. If he has any problem, it is more likely to be the problem of his continuing identification with Negroes as a group. He is usually a "first" Negro to have achieved this or that distinction. Because of this, he occupies a special place on both sides of the racial line and only most rarely can he manage to ignore this fact.
Harold R. Isaacs, *The New World of Negro Americans*[1]

Solomon Carter Fuller made the decision to retire from Boston University's School of Medicine in 1933, when a white assistant professor was promoted to full professor and appointed head of the Neurology Department. During his last five years at the university, Fuller had served as the head of the department, but was never officially given the title. Despite his 34 years of exemplary teaching and research, he had never been promoted beyond the rank of associate professor. Rather than contesting the appointment, Fuller chose to leave the university.

> I thoroughly dislike publicity of that sort and despise sympathy. I regard life as a battle in which we win or lose. As far as I am concerned, to be vanquished, if not ingloriously is not so bad after all. With the sort of work that I have done, I might have gone farther and reached a higher plan had it not been for my color.[2]

Upon his retirement from Boston University, Fuller received the title of Professor Emeritus of Neurology, a designation that was renewed on an annual basis for the remainder of his life. Still, there would always remain a sense of frustration that he had never received his well-earned academic recognition in the medical school or advancement in the Massachusetts State Hospital system because of the color of his skin. At the time of Fuller's resignation, professional restrictions continued to exist for black physicians. Many hospitals refused to grant them staff privileges. Membership in the American Medical Association was limited to those who had been accepted to their local county medical associations. If their local group would not accept their application for membership, then the national association would reject them.[3]

Like many other middle-class black intellectuals, Fuller was alienated from the culture of the African American population. His son, Solomon, Jr. felt that his father's privileged professional status also contributed to his detachment from other blacks. He recalled his father's disapproval of his brother Tom's marriage to a woman who was a waitress with little education.

> I always felt a superiority that came from my upbringing. I was brought up in an elite environment and did not understand black culture. For instance, I did not know that there was such a thing as colored time. I was told to meet a colored friend in Philadelphia and arrived promptly at the time we had planned. When he showed up late he was surprised at my remarks regarding his lateness.
>
> When my brother and I graduated from college, we began to realize what our attitudes had been toward other blacks and we were ashamed. So my brother, who was a great card player, decided to have a card party when my folks were away and invited all black men. It was a disaster, because their behavior we couldn't tolerate.[4]

Fuller encouraged his sons to go to a white college, with the hope that it would prepare them to be successful in a white-dominated society. Solomon, Jr. and Tom went to Colby College in Maine (May Bragg's alma mater), while Perry studied art in New York. Fuller's sons felt a great deal of pressure from the high expectations placed upon them by their father.

> Father wanted me to go to medical school. I attended Colby College, but was not good at academics. I think I had learning disabilities. I did excel in track. I never felt that I could live up to my father's expectations and didn't get close to him until he became blind eight years before his death.[5]

Although none of Fuller's sons chose to follow their father's path in medicine, all three were successful in their selected fields. Solomon, Jr. became a field scout executive for the Boy Scouts of America and later held an executive position at the United Community Services in Boston. Tom joined the Air Force and was stationed at the Tuskegee Air Base. When his military service ended, he moved back to Framingham, went into the automobile business, and later became the first black licensed broker on the Boston Stock Exchange, working for Merrill Lynch. Perry, who inherited his mother's artistic talent, became a sculptor.

Fuller constantly advised his children to maintain decorum and high moral standards. He was unable to accept his youngest son, Perry's, homosexuality and was concerned with the impact that it might have on his family, at a time when society viewed homosexual acts between men as criminal behavior. Solomon, Jr. remembered his brother as a successful artist, but also as someone who could not take care of himself and was always getting into trouble. He had been jailed for assault and had a notorious reputation.

> He was more than a homosexual, he was a deviant. But it might be that if we had accepted him as a homosexual, that he wouldn't have been a deviant. What a tragedy it is that we weren't prepared to accept homosexuals.[6]

Perry was a great disappointment to Solomon and the cause of dissension with Meta, who loved her son dearly. When Fuller was diagnosed with diabetes, the stress of dealing with Perry's behavior began to have a detrimental effect on his health. To help his father, Solomon, Jr. agreed to take his brother away to New York.

> We were proud people. Perry had to be disposed of, otherwise our whole family would suffer. Because we knew of his shenanigans, we were afraid of him. So that was one of the things he held over us. Several years later, I was living at the YMCA in Harlem at the time, and I don't know how we got together in Greenwich Village, but we did somehow. I was about 39 or 40. He asked, 'Could you give me a ride to Philadelphia?' Immediately, I flinched. I was afraid to do anything with him because of his history, but there was no way that I could say no. I said 'I don't want any shenanigans,' cause I didn't know what he was up to. We got to Elizabeth, New Jersey. He directed me to a building and said, 'Sol, could you give me some time here?' I said, 'Ok, but I'm leaving you right here.' In about 15 – 20 minutes, he came out of the building and said, 'Come on in.' I refused to come in, so he went and got a man to beckon me in. And this man looked very important, so I went in. It was an aviation shop. Apparently Perry had sold some drawings to some aviation company and had won the confidence of this man. On the way back, I asked Perry, 'So how long have you known this man? He answered, 'Oh, I saw his name in a magazine. It was the first time I ever met him.'[7]

Perry went on to become a successful artist and inventor, exhibiting his work in New York City. In addition to creating reproductions of African masks, he also designed automobiles and airplanes. He was reported to have worked on Amelia Earhart's plane. Perry died of AIDS disease at the age of 74.

While her sons were growing up, Meta worked as a volunteer in many political and community activities, including the Women's Peace Party and the Equal Suffrage Movement. She later became disillusioned with the suffrage movement when she realized that while white women had achieved the right to vote, many blacks were still denied that right. In a presentation on "The Negro in Art" at Framingham's Grace Church, she reminded the audience of the racial inequality that still existed in American society.

> All the world is interested at the present time in treasures of art and of ancient handicraft that is being taken from the tomb of a Negro king. Yet, the Negro is being rated as the lowest on the scale of social development. The life of the Negro in the South and even in some parts of the North can be said to be a community within a community.[8]

With money inherited from her mother, Meta bought a lot on Larner's Pond, a quarter mile from the Fullers' home. It was on this picturesque site overlooking the northeast corner of Larner's Pond that she built her studio in 1929, without her husband's knowledge. Solomon, Jr. remembered that his father was upset when he first learned of Meta's studio, but that he eventually accepted her decision to move her studio out of the house because of his concern that the dust in the small, confined attic would ruin her health. Meta intended her studio to be a tribute to the members of her family who had contributed to her development as an artist.

> It had two beautiful fireplaces and an ideal atmosphere. There I did much work. I held classes and the like. Friends and neighbors loved to congregate there, and came from near and far to sit by the open fire, chat and sip tea when I had open house. I had many open houses for my friends, put on special Christmas exhibits, and so forth... It was my hope to preserve it as a, shall I say, shrine – one to which people would come after my demise and witness whatever message my work might proclaim...Fate deemed otherwise.[9]

Fuller's ties to his family in his native country, Liberia, had been severed in 1924 when he became a United States citizen. His brother, Thomas, who was later assassinated while serving as the mayor of Monrovia, disowned and declared him "dead" when he received word of Solomon's U.S. citizenship. In the 35 years following Fuller's immigration to the United States, Liberia had experienced large-scale government corruption and financial crises. By 1904, European colonial expansion had resulted in a reduction of 75 percent of the country's territory. To prevent further colonization, Liberia's president, Arthur Barclay (who was married to Fuller's cousin) extended citizenship to the country's indigenous population. A tax imposed on all citizens added to the financial hardship that already existed as a result of a British monopoly of the country's exports. In a letter dated June 21, 1916, Thomas Fuller requested money from his brother, Solomon, to help care for their mother.

> Doctor says she don't need no medisen. She needs a tonic and good nourishment. I trys my best but times are so hard now. Since the war no money...Steamers call here wonce a month and things has got to a crisis. Now that the English government only allows things to be shipted from England to Liberia to only 5 firms...The four of the firms are white. English, French, Duchman, only one Liberian allowed to git goods from England now. You can see from this how we are sufing. I am a shame to say I am hard up. Send me something to help keep Mother up. We who are working in the government are working on promises. No money, no revenue and it is a hard job for the Government to meet 1/3 of her demand. Whatever you send when things git better, I will return same. If it were not for Mother sake I would not aske from you for help. I am trying to live off my farm but it is not enuf to sell to git ready cash to buy nourishment for mother.[10]

Fuller received word of his mother's death from her pastor in 1921. Although he no longer had any contact from his Liberian relatives, the Fullers often entertained visitors from Liberia. In 1919, Charles D.B. King, the president-elect of Liberia, and his wife visited the Fullers in Framingham. He and Fuller had grown up together in Liberia. King later went on to serve as president of Liberia from 1920 to 1932, resigning after his administration was condemned by the League of Nations' for their involvement in the Fernando Po scheme. In the scheme, a deal was negotiated between Liberian politicians, national security forces, village chiefs, and government officials and the Firestone Company that resulted in the forced transportation of several thousand Liberian workers to rubber plantations on the island of Fernando Po (later known as Bioko, Equatorial Guinea). Many of the workers died from the poor working conditions and tropical diseases.[11]

Liberian students who were studying at New England colleges were also frequent guests at the Fuller's home.

> There was a man who had made his way through school in Liberia and came to the U. S. to go to college. This man would come and stay with us on weekends. And we, with our New England attitudes would suggest that he might mow the lawn for us. Rather reluctantly, he agreed, but did such a poor job, that he was not asked again. Whether that was deliberate or not, we don't know. He graduated with a degree in civil engineering and went back to Liberia. Many years later, when a friend went over and visited him, he reported that this man had not been able to accomplish his goal of building a road system in Liberia – only one-half mile of the road had been completed.[12]

The religious beliefs instilled in Fuller through his maternal grandparents' missionary experience during his early years in Liberia had been challenged by his moral standards about fairness and equality upon his arrival in the United

States. His faith continued to wither as a result of the hypocrisy and racial intolerance that he witnessed in America. He was displeased with his wife and sons' involvement in the church and urged them to carefully examine the church's teachings in relation to the facts. "He never would go to church based upon an incident in which he was told by a woman in church one day that he was sitting in her husband's seat. All my teen years I tried to get dad to come to the church," said his son Solomon, Jr. "But I didn't succeed."[13] Although Fuller would not attend church, many of the town's ministers would come to visit him to share their intellectual and spiritual views.

> My father had great spiritual qualities. People came to him for a spiritual communion that was a refreshing, inspiring, and motivating experience. Some people kept coming back to him – right up to the time of his death – not for treatment of a mental disorder, but just to have a spiritual exchange with quieting personality that it had a great calming effect on his patient's problems.[14]

In the years since the Fullers moved into their house on Warren Road, Framingham had continued to grow and prosper. In the early 1930s, the Depression brought the loss of jobs for many of the town's residents, but the town had recovered and was now a manufacturing center surrounded by farmland. Solomon and Meta had become well-known and respected members of their community. Meta was active in several of the town's women's and drama clubs and was often the only nonwhite member. Meta's annual exhibition of her work, begun in 1930, had become a community event. Framingham residents remember seeing Solomon in his later years, a thin man with grey hair and a small grey beard, walking down Union Avenue dressed in a suit and a Panama hat.

One of Fuller's closest friends in his later years was William Hinton, with whom he shared an interest in gardening. An African-American physician, who was known for developing a blood test for the diagnosis of syphilis, Dr. Hinton had also experienced the barriers of racism in his practice of medicine. Although he had received his medical degree from Harvard, taught at Harvard's medical school, and written the first medical textbook by an African–American (*Syphilis and Its Treatment*), he was not allowed to treat patients in Boston hospitals. A rivalry developed between Fuller and Hinton as to who could produce the best flowers. Fuller's son, Solomon, Jr. remembered "Hinton used to say, 'Fuller, I'm going to put your eyes out' – meaning with the beauty of the flowers he meant to grow. Dad would make some laughing reply, but they both loved flowers and were serious about growing them."[15]

Fuller's old friend May Bragg had married Arthur Weston, a local surgeon, in 1905 and moved to Keene, New Hampshire, where Dr. Weston became the town's surgeon and football coach. She gave birth to a daughter, Ruth, in 1911. Fuller was a frequent guest at the Weston home, arriving in "a great big car" and often staying overnight. The Weston's daughter remembers, "My father would take Dr. Fuller to dinner in Keene and on many occasions was told by the manager of the restaurant that he would not seat Dr. Fuller because he was colored."[16]

> Dad would take a week's vacation and visit the Westons. Dr. Weston was so preoccupied with his practice that they couldn't get together until the wee hours. So during the day, Mrs. Weston had to take care of Dad. They would go visit old places together. Following Dr. Weston's death, Dad would visit Mrs. Weston frequently and she would often come to stay with us.[17]

May's daughter has fond memories of Dr. Fuller and recounted the time when she was seriously ill with a breast abscess. Fuller made arrangements for her to be treated at a Boston hospital and accompanied her on the train to her home in Keene when she was discharged. She also remembers her visits to Framingham.

> Mrs. Fuller was putting on a play and invited mother and me. We arrived late, the lights had dimmed and the show was starting. When the lights went on, we looked around and discovered that we were the only white people in the audience.[18]

Fuller had continued to work as a consultant at Westborough State Hospital and Framingham's Marlboro Hospital, as well as the Pennsylvania State Hospital in Allentown until 1939, when his eyesight began to fail. He had been diagnosed with diabetes when he was in his forties and was a patient at the Joslin Diabetes Center in Boston. By 1942, Fuller had lost most of his sight and could no longer engage in one of his greatest pleasures – reading. His sons and friends read to him and he listened to music and to the radio. At that time, the selection of talking books for the blind was limited and not available on the topics that were of interest to Fuller. His attempts to tend to his garden were unsuccessful as the weeds eventually took over. His book-binding, photography, and laboratory work were no longer possible. His disability and dependency on his family brought about a closer relationship with his oldest son. Solomon, Jr. would drive him around town and listen to his father's stories about his ancestors, his life in Liberia, and the famous people that he had known in medicine.

Wanting to see his grandchildren again before he became totally blind, Solomon and Meta traveled to the Tuskegee Air Base to visit Tom and his family. Both Tom and his brother, Solomon, Jr., along with their families, had lived for short periods of time in their parents' home. According to his grandson, John Lewis Fuller, Solomon was very strict with his grandchildren, insisting on a quiet, orderly household. The children were not allowed to be in the house on summer days, and when they were in the house, they were expected to be well behaved. Despite his blindness, Fuller was able to identify which grandchildren and neighborhood children were in the house. As with his sons, Fuller emphasized the importance of education to his grandchildren –

Though growing old, Dr. Fuller still acted like an eager young medical student as he talked with me about the newest ideas and methods of treating mental illness. Talking with Dr. Fuller was a great education for me because he had worked and studied with the great minds in 20th.century psychiatry and psychoanalysis. In an era when the professional development of black people was discouraged and inadequately rewarded, Dr. Fuller persevered until he secured the finest training available.[22]

In 1943, fifty years after his graduation from Livingstone College, Fuller returned to his alma mater for the dedication of the Price Memorial Building, the school's new science center. During the commencement ceremonies, he was awarded an honorary degree of Doctor of Science and proclaimed one of the school's outstanding graduates. In a radio interview by Professor Clarence W. Wright of the Biology Department at Livingstone, Fuller was asked about the impact of World War II on the mental state of soldiers and civilians. He responded by explaining the government's programs to screen military trainees for nervous or mental diseases and to rehabilitate veterans suffering from combat induced mental disorders. He also expressed the opinion that the war, while a source of much stress on civilians, could also have the effect of boosting their morale.[23]

During World War I, Fuller had developed an interest in the study of the disturbance to the nervous system related to battle, known as "shell shock".[24]Also referred to as "battle fatigue", "conversion hysteria", "exhaustion neurosis", and during the Second World War, "war neurosis", the condition was treated with rest, sedatives, and counseling.

The years following the Second World War saw the emergence of a civil rights movement. Public sentiment in the United States against racial superiority had been influenced by Hitler's treatment of Jews, blacks, and other non-Aryan groups, and by Mussolini's invasion of Ethiopia. In 1941, A. Philip Randolph organized a march on Washington which led to President Roosevelt's executive order establishing the Fair Employment Practices Commission. Desegregation of the military was ordered in 1948 by President Truman and the mandate for change was carried out by Eisenhower during his Presidency.[25] Black physicians and other health care professionals continued their fight for equality in professional organizations, schools and hospitals. White physicians in increasing numbers demonstrated their support for the admission of black physicians to the American Medical Association and one by one, the Association's state chapters voted to accept blacks as members. Meanwhile, the members of the National Association for the Advancement of Colored People (NAACP) continued to seek change through the courts and Congress with little success. The fight for racial equality gained momentum when the Democratic Party, led by President Truman, incorporated the precept of non-discrimination into proposed legislation. But Solomon Carter Fuller would not live to see the results of that legislation, which culminated in the landmark decision of the Supreme Court on school desegregation in May 1954.

Fuller died on January 16, 1953 at the Framingham Union Hospital at the age of 80, following a long battle with diabetes mellitus and gastrointestinal cancer. His dear friend, May Weston, had received word of his impending death and rushed to his bedside. She patted his check and they said their good-byes in Latin. Dr. James Ayer, a close friend, also visited him shortly before his death.

> I saw and talked with him: though blind, his memory was excellent, his speech flawless, his interests alive. He knew he had not long to live, but accepted the fact in his usual philosophical manner, like the perfect gentlemen he was.[26]

Fuller's ashes were spread in Martha's Vineyard Sound following a small service. The family was not prepared for the number of people who wanted to pay their respects. Solomon, Jr. noted that many people had expressed their disappointment that they were not invited to the funeral.

Meta had put her sculpture aside to care for her husband during his last years, leaving her studio in the hands of a former student. Her days were long and her time spent between her caregiving duties and evening art classes at the studio. At the time of his death, she was 75 and emotionally and physically exhausted. Soon after, Meta was diagnosed with tuberculosis and spent the next two years in the Middlesex County Sanitarium. When she entered the sanitarium, she turned her studio over to her son, Tom, where he lived with his wife and three children. Upon her discharge, Meta returned to her home where Solomon, Jr. and his family had been living. Her studio had been sold while she was away, so her son set up a small bedroom on the second floor of her house and she resumed her sculpting.

Soon, she began to exhibit her sculpture in Boston area exhibits and received several commissions for her work. It was in the years that followed Solomon Carter Fuller's death that Meta found the admiration and respect for her art that had often been denied to her. The nature of Solomon and Meta's marriage had been that of mutual respect, but with some deference to Solomon's view of a wife's role. While Meta assumed that role, she also struggled to be a person in her own right, rather than an extension of her husband.

Meta also returned to her church after her husband's death. A life-long Episcopalian, she had been disassociated from the church for many years because of racial discrimination. Her religion now became a source of comfort and much of her art in her later years focused on religious themes.

In 1961, Meta won a prize of $500 and a silver medal for her work that was featured in the exhibition, "New Vistas in American Art", which marked the opening of a new fine arts building at Howard University. "The work of Meta Fuller," the program noted, "represents the best in the tradition of American sculpture."[27] Meta was given the use of a studio in Boston where she conducted classes and exhibited her work. Many of her works can be found in churches and public buildings in Framingham, including the town's hospital and library. She also wrote poetry, something that she began while a patient in the tuberculosis sanitarium. In 1962, Meta was awarded the honorary degree of Doctor of Letters from Livingstone College, her husband's alma mater. Twelve years earlier, she had traveled to Livingstone to present its president, William J. Trent, with a plaque of his likeness in recognition of the 25th anniversary of his presidency.

In addition to awards for her art, Meta was also recognized for her focus on civil rights. In 1965, she was awarded a citation of merit by the Boston chapter of the National Association for the Advancement of Colored People for her contribution to the cause of civil rights and human freedom through the art of sculpture. During the early 1960s, Meta had donated pieces of her sculpture to raise money for the voter registration campaigns in the South. Although she considered herself a feminist, and had been active in the fight for the right to vote for women, she had not previously been actively involved in the civil rights movement. A very quiet and proud woman whose demeanor was influenced by her upbringing, she expressed her anger and frustration at American society's treatment of blacks in her art. She was not optimistic that change in social conditions for blacks would occur in the near future because she felt that American society would not tolerate a growth in the political and social awareness in the black population.[28]

Meta Vaux Warrick Fuller died on March 13, 1968 at Cushing Hospital in Framingham, fifteen years after the death of her husband. She was approaching her 91st birthday and had been in failing health during her last year. Her funeral was held at St. Andrew's Episcopal Church in Framingham and her ashes joined those of her husband in Martha's Vineyard Sound.

Departure

The time is near (reluctance laid aside)
I see the barge afloat upon the ebbing tide,
While on the shores my friends and loved ones stand.
I wave to them a cheerful parting hand;
Then take my place with Charon at the helm,
And turn and wave again to them.
Oh, may the voyage not be arduous nor long,
But echoing with chant and joyful song,
May I behold with reverence and grace,
The wonderous vision of the Master's face.

Meta Vaux Warrick Fuller
Framingham's Women's Club, 1964

Chapter 10

Recognition of Accomplishments
Boston
1976

Where My Caravan Rested

In many ways life has dealt kindly with me, beginning, I have been told, as a delicate youngster. I have lived a reasonably long journey, and since puberty have been free from any long disabling illness. I have seen my children grow to manhood and have been further blessed in the happiness of grandchildren. I have made many friendships. Through the years I have tried to make the best of my opportunities though no doubt failing many times and have enjoyed the work that for which I was trained. What more then could one ask. Yet human nature is such that complete satisfaction is seldom attainable and that perhaps is a good trait.[1]

Solomon Carter Fuller

Sadly, the recognition of Solomon Carter Fuller's accomplishments did not come until many years after his death. In April 1976, the Dr. Solomon Carter Fuller Mental Health Center opened its doors with Fuller's son, Solomon, Jr., participating in the ribbon-cutting ceremony.[2] The ten-story building, located adjacent to Boston University Medical Center was designed to provide facilities for psychiatric outpatient services, community education, and research. A bust of Fuller, a bronze version of the original sculpture made by Meta in their Framingham home, sits in the center's lobby. The center was named for Fuller by an act of the Massachusetts Legislature to honor his achievements in

neuropsychiatry and his promotion of better mental health care for minorities and the poor.

The impetus for this honor began in 1973 when the School of Medicine's Division of Psychiatry organized a "Solomon Carter Fuller Day" during Boston University's centennial celebration. Dr. Charles Pinderhughes, a Professor of Psychiatry at the school and a former student of Fuller's, had led the effort to honor Fuller.[3]   The day-long tribute featured presentations on the status of modern psychiatry by leaders in the mental health field. Donations were made to have the bust of Dr. Fuller cast in bronze. The center became a reality through the collaborative efforts of the local, state and national associations for mental health, the Boston University Division of Psychiatry, and local community organizations.

The state of science and medicine at the time of the Dr. Solomon Carter Fuller Center's opening was very different from that of Fuller's era. Science was now considered a national priority in the United States and most medical research was being conducted in universities instead of hospital laboratories, supported by government and private foundation funding. Psychiatry had moved into the mainstream of American medicine and the prevention of mental illness had become a social issue.[4]

In the years leading up to the dedication of the Dr. Solomon Carter Fuller Mental Health Center, Fuller's accomplishments had also begun to be recognized by medical professionals in Boston and at the national level. In 1953, the year of Fuller's death and over 40 years after Fuller had published his article stating his theory that Alzheimer's disease was probably caused by something other than arteriosclerosis, medical researchers confirmed his findings.[5]

In 1966, realizing that Fuller had not received the acknowledgment he deserved for his distinguished teaching, scientific productivity, and clinical excellence, the National Medical Association's Psychiatry and Neurology Section named him as a role model for black physicians in promoting positive images and striving for excellence in science and medicine.

Dr. Charles Prudhomme, the first African-American to hold an office in the American Psychiatric Association, and his wife presented a portrait of Dr. Fuller to the Association in 1972, in a ceremony that recognized Fuller as the first black psychiatrist in the United States and one of the "great men of American psychiatry." The portrait, painted by Naida Willette Page from the National Medical Association, hangs on the wall in the Association's national headquarters in Washington, D.C.

The Solomon Fuller Institute was also established that year by the Black Psychiatrists of America, with Dr. Robert H. Sharply of the Harvard Medical School as its director. Its international membership was comprised of medical scientists who were interested in the relationship between social issues and mental health. The private non-profit organization's goal was to promote and develop education and research in psychiatry with an emphasis on minority populations. Several years later, the Institute closed due to the lack of funds.

Fuller lived during a period in history when science was often used in an attempt to demonstrate the inferiority of black people. That Fuller's accomplishments have been significant in the advancement of science and medicine, in spite of the obstacles and lack of opportunities as a result of the racism that existed in the United States during this period, is a testimonial to his ability and perseverance. But, according to his son, Solomon, Jr., he would have never wanted to be known only as "the first black neuropathologist" or "the first black psychiatrist."[6] Unlike his wife, Meta, Solomon had never been an outspoken activist for injustice and social change. His battles against prejudice were fought quietly and through academic excellence.

Of all the honors bestowed upon Solomon and Meta Fuller, there is one that has great irony. On April 2, 1995, eighty-six years after their neighbors tried to prevent the couple from building a home in Framingham, the town dedicated a school in their honor. The school, formerly Framingham South High School, is located a few blocks from the Fuller home, and many of the Fullers' grandchildren had attended classes there. As their family gathered on the stage of the Fuller Middle School, they heard public officials speak of the Fullers' contributions to the town. "The Fullers' demonstrated to the town of Framingham as well as to the Commonwealth what a family can do when it works together and focuses on education," said Pablo Calderon, Executive Director for Minority Business for the state of Massachusetts, who was tutored in English by Meta when he was growing up in Framingham. She was "the person who taught me English and also taught me to respect myself and respect others." But, perhaps the most significant remarks made at the ceremony were those of the school's principal, Juan Rodriguez, when he said that he hoped that the children who came to the school would learn the stories behind the building's name. "We should say first, how grateful we are that they chose to live and work among us in our town."[7]

Epilogue

Washington, D.C.
2001

Fuller would have been proud of the accomplishments of his descendants. Many carry on his legacy of a love for education and this country.

The terrorist attack on September 11, 2001 was recorded as the second bloodiest day in United States history, second only to the Civil War Battle of Antietam. The impact of the attack on the Pentagon that day was particularly devastating for the Fuller family. Among the 184 victims was the granddaughter of Solomon and Meta Fuller. Named for her grandmother, Meta Louis Fuller Waller was a special programs coordinator for the Secretary of the United States Army and had an office in the Pentagon. A graduate of Harvard University's Kennedy School of Government, she was in charge of fundraising for a foundation for the Army's humanitarian projects.

Meta had just returned from a trip to Africa and called her mother from the airport to let her know that she had arrived safely. "I had been so worried about her the whole time that she was in Africa and was relieved when I knew that she was back in the United States," said her mother, Harriet Fuller. "I told her to take a few days off from work and to get some rest, but she said that she had to go into the office and get some work done first."[1]

Meta was in her office when the plane hit the Pentagon the morning of September 11. She was reported missing for a week. Throughout that time, her family kept calling her cell phone, which continued to ring with no answer. When Meta's remains were found, DNA testing was performed to confirm her identity. The autopsy reports states that she died from blunt trauma. Two years after her daughter's death, Harriet Fuller still finds it difficult to find closure to her grief. In her home, along with Meta's cremated remains, is a stuffed monkey that Meta brought to her mother from her trip to Africa.

Solomon Carter Fuller maintained the belief that his education and professional accomplishments would allow him to be treated fairly and with respect, and he instilled this belief in his children and grandchildren. Many members of the new generations of the Fuller family have become educators, carrying on his legacy. The story that began with courage of a freed slave, John Lewis Fuller, continues to inspire others today.

> None of his descendants have been great people, as the World measures greatness, but I think most of them have been good citizens of their communities, but I think most of them have contributed to civic life to the extent of their abilities.[2]
>
> Solomon Carter Fuller

Appendix

Publications of Solomon Carter Fuller

1. Four cases of pernicious anemia among insane subjects. *New England Medical Gazette*, 1901.
2. The effects of Belladonna upon animal tissue. Chapter VII, in H. P. Bellows, (ed.), *Test Drug Proving*. O. O' and I. Society.
3. A study of the neurofibrils in dementia paralytica, dementia senilis chronic alcoholism, cerebral lues and microcephalic idiocy. *American Journal of Insanity*, 1907; 63, pp. 415-68.
4. Report of a case of delirium tremens, with autopsy. *Proc. Soc. Neurol. Psychiat.*, 1907.
5. An analysis of 100 cases of dementia precox in men. *Proc. Soc. Neurol. Psychiat.* 1908.
6. Cerebral histology with special reference to histopathology of the psychoses. Special lecture before the Department of Biology, Clark University, Worcester, MA, 1909.
7. Preliminary report of four cases of aphasia with serial sections throughout the entire brain in three. *New Eng. Soc. Psychiat.*, 1909.
8. Involutional melancholia. *New Eng. Soc. Psychiat.*, 1910.
9. Neurofibrils in manic-depressive insanity. Manic-Depressive Symposium. *New Eng. Soc. Psychiat.*, 1910.
10. An analysis of 3,140 admissions to Westborough State Hospital, with reference to the diagnosis of involutional melancholia. *Pro. Soc. Neurol. Psychiat.*, 1911.
11. A study of the military plaques found in brains of the aged. *American Journal of Insanity*, 1911; 68, pp. 147-220.
12. Further observations on Alzheimer's disease. (with H.I. Klopp). *American Journal of Insanity*, 1912; 69, pp. 17-29.
13. Alzheimer's disease (senium praecox): The report of a case and review of published cases. *Journal of Nervous and Mental Disease*, 1912, pp. 440-55.
14. Amyloid degeneration of the brain in two cases of general paresis. The Proceedings of the American Medico-Psychological Association, Sixty-Ninth Annual Meeting, Niagara Falls, Canada, June 10-13, 1913.
15. Histopathological alteration in cellular neuroglia and fibrillary mesoblastic components of cerebral cortical interstitium. *Boston Med. & S. J.*, 1924; 190, pp. 314-322.

Notes

Preface

1. R. Ellison, *Shadow and Act*, New York: Random House, 1964, p. 123.

Introduction: Fuller's Arrival in Germany, 1905

1. R. Ellison, *Shadow and Act*, New York: Random House, 1964, p. 315.
2. "A new psychiatric clinic" This clinic was later called the Max Planck Institute.
3. For further reading on European influence on American medicine, see *Encyclopedia of the History of Medicine*, by W.F. Bynum and R. Porter (eds.), New York: Routledge, 1993.
4. Solomon Carter Fuller's notes, (1950).
5. Ibid.
6. Ibid.
7. Ibid.

Chapter 1. The Beginning: John Lewis Fuller, Norfolk, Virginia, 1830

1. J. Dunford, "One man's 50's". A review of Mel Watkins, *Dancing with Strangers: A Memoir*, *New York Times Book Review*, February 15, 1998.
2. Solomon Fuller. In a letter to Luther P. Jackson, Virginia State College, Petersburg, Virginia, March 27, 1950.
3. According to the 1782 Virginia law, a slave owner could free a slave by going to the courthouse, stating the reason for freeing the slave, and renouncing all claims to the slave. When the deed of manumission was signed and witnessed, the slave was officially a free person. See Tommy Bogger, *Free Blacks in Norfolk, Virginia, 1790–1860*, Charlottesville, VA: University Press of Virginia, 1997, p. 8.
4. Virginia differentiated between white indentured and black servants, making the length of service for whites shorter and defining their legal rights more clearly. From Eric Foner, *America's Black Past*, New York: Harper & Row, 1970, p. 497.
5. Solomon Fuller's notes, 1950.
6. The Jarratt family home is included in the listing of African-American Historic Sites in Petersburg, Virginia. Located on Pocahontas Island, the house was built circa 1820.
7. A history of the Jarratt family can be found in Luther Jackson, "Free Negroes of Petersburg, Virginia." *The Journal of Negro History*, Vol. XII, pp. 367-68.
8. Frederick Douglas, *Life and Times of Frederick Douglas*. New York: Collier Books, 1892, p. 208.
9. In 1830, there were an estimated 319,000 free Negroes in the United States. From John Hope Franklin, *From Slavery to Freedom*, New York: Knopf, 1967.
10. When the Black Laws of 1832 were passed, Virginia required free Negroes to register. A patrol system was organized that mandated free Negroes and slaves

to show their freedom papers to county police upon demand. The right was given to patrolmen to jail any black person who could not give a satisfactory account of himself. Curfew time was usually ten o'clock and any black found traveling after that time was subject to a lashing and imprisonment. In addition to patrolmen, every white citizen was granted the power to apprehend blacks. See Workers of the Writers' Program of the Works Projects Administration, State of Virginia, *The Negro in Virginia* (New York: Hastings House, 1940, p. 142; Philip Foner, *History of Black Americans,* Westport, CT: Greenwood Press, 1975, pp. 510–12; and Ira Berlin, *Slaves without Masters*, New York: The New Press, 1974, p. 244.

11. Fuller, Ibid., 1950.
12. Douglas, Ibid., p. 164.
13. In 1831, the Virginia General Assembly passed a law that outlawed all meetings of free Negroes that were held to teach them reading and writing skills. Other changes that affected the economic status of free Negroes were the depressed economy caused by the embargo of 1807 and the increasing numbers of European immigrants that began arriving in Norfolk in the 1830s. From Tommy Bogger, *Free Blacks in Norfolk, Virginia, 1790–1860,* Charlottesville, VA: University Press of Virginia, 1997.
14. In 1816, the Virginia legislature adopted a resolution authorizing the Governor to contact the President of the United States for the purpose of obtaining a territory outside of the United States to "serve for an asylum of such persons of colour as are now free, and may desire the same, and for those who may hereafter be emancipated within the commonwealth." From Archibald Alexander, *A History of Colonization on the Western Coast of Africa,* New York: Negro Universities Press, 1969, pp. 76-77. For additional information on the development of the American Colonization Society, see Amos Beyan, *The American Colonization Society and the Creation of The Liberian State,* Lanham, MD: University Press of America, 1991; Philip Fowler, *History of Black Americans,* Westport, CT: Greenwood Press, 1975; and Yekutiel Gersoni, *Black Colonialism*, Boulder, CO: Westview Press, 1985.
15. Solomon Fuller, Ibid., 1950.
16. Norfolk City Marriage Bonds, No. 8, 1848–1850.
17. Solomon Fuller, Ibid., 1950.

Chapter 2. A New Life in Africa: Monrovia, 1852

1. Solomon Carter Fuller's notes, 1950.
2. The original superintendent of the Liberian colony, Jehudi Ashmun, is buried in a cemetery located in New Haven, Connecticut, across from Yale University.
3. Fuller, Ibid., 1950.
4. Ibid., 1950.
5. The United States did not recognize the new country until 1862 because of its reluctance to accredit a black diplomat in Washington. From I. Bell Wiley (ed.) *Slaves No More: Letters From Liberia, 1833–1869*, Lexington, KY: University of Kentucky Press, 1980, p. 2. For additional information on the establishment of Liberia, see Yekutiel Gersoni, *Black Colonialism*, Boulder, CO: Westview Press, 1985; D. Elwood Dunn & Svend Holsoe, *The Historical Dictionary of Liberia,* Lanham, MD: Scarecrow Press, Inc., 1985; and C.

Abayomi Cassell, *Liberia: History of the First African Republic*, New York: Fountainhead Publications, 1970.

6.   "The Charitable Mechanics Society of Monrovia was a society something like the Masons – like a protective club and it was started with the idea of taking care of retired mechanics, the feeble and sick and things of that sort" Fuller, Ibid., 1950.

7.   In 1856, the existence of the state of Maryland was threatened by bloody conflict between native tribes and settlers. A treaty was negotiated by Joseph Jenkins Roberts, Liberia's Commissioner and Minister to Maryland and by Dr. James Hall, founder of the colony. It was at this time that the people of Maryland realized that they could not continue to safely exist as an independent state and they decided to join Liberia. From C. Abayomi Cassell, *Liberia: History of the First African Republic*. New York: Fountainhead Publications, 1970.

8.   Fuller, Ibid., 1950.

9.   A settler's account of life in Liberia in 1953 can be found in W. Nesbit & S. Williams, *Two Black Views of Liberia*, New York: Arno Press & The New York Times, 1969.

10.   Fuller, Ibid., 1950.

11.   Ibid., 1950.

12.   In 1870, there were an estimated 7,000–10,000 Liberians of American origin. From R. West, *Back to Africa*, London: Jonathan Cape, Ltd., 1970, p. 221.

13.   In 1874, limited African participation in the legislature was permitted when the government decided to allow two chiefs from each county to act as advisors. From Yekutiel Gershoni, *Black Colonialism*. Boulder, CO: Westview Press, 1985, p. 23.

14.   Article 20 of the original Liberian Constitution stated, "There shall be no slavery in the Commonwealth." From C.C. Boone, *Liberia As I Know It*, Westport, CT: Negro Universities Press, 1970, p. 71.

15.   Solomon Carter Fuller, Jr., 1998.

16.   By 1900, the price of Liberian coffee had dropped from twenty-four cents to four cents a pound and the volume of coffee exported had decreased 50 percent. In West, Ibid. 1970, pp. 253-4.

17.   Observation by T. McCants Stewart in Gershoni, Ibid. 1985.

18.   Liberia College was closed in 1895 by the President of Liberia, James J. Cheeseman. The college was later reopened in 1899. From Cassell, Ibid., 1970, p. 367.

Chapter 3. In Pursuit of a Dream: North Carolina, 1889

1.   John Hope Franklin, *From Slavery to Freedom*, 4th ed. New York: Knopf, 1984, pp. 250-53.

2.   From Solomon Carter Fuller's speech to the Livingstone College graduating class of 1943, upon acceptance of an honorary degree fifty years after his own graduation from the college.

3.   Ibid., 1943.

4.   W. F. Fonvielle, *Reminiscences of College Days*, Goldsboro, NC: Edwards & Broughton, 1904.

5. Owen J. McNamara, "Solomon Carter Fuller." In *Centerscope Magazine*, Winter, 1976.
6. In 1895, of the 385 Negro physicians who received a medical degree in the United States, only 27 graduated from white medical schools. From H.M. Morais, *The History of the Negro in Medicine.* The Association for the Study of Negro Life and History. New York: Publishers Co, 1967.
7. Robert H. Sharpley, on Solomon Carter Fuller in George E. Gifford Jr. (ed.), *Psychoanalysis, Psychotherapy and the New England Medical Scene, 1894-1944.* New York: Science History Publications, 1978, p. 183.
8. William Malamud, Psychiatric Therapies, in The American Psychiatric Association's *One Hundred Years of American Psychiatry*, New York: Columbia University Press, 1944, p. 303.
9. Arthur Mann, *Yankee Reformers in the Urban Age*, Cambridge, MA, 1954, pp. 1-5.
10. Fuller, Ibid., 1943.

Chapter 4. Learning and Teaching: Boston, 1897

1. C. King. *Fire in My Bones*. Grand Rapids, MI: W.E. Eerdmann Publishing Co., 1983, p. 271.
2. Henry Hurd (Ed.), *Mental Illness and Social Policy, Vol. II.*, Arno Press, New York, 1973. A reprint of the 1916 edition published by Johns Hopkins Press, Baltimore, pp. 718-24.
3. Solomon Carter Fuller's notes, 1950.
4. Ibid., 1950.
5. Ibid., 1950
6. For further reading on the treatment of mental illness in the mid-19th century, see Sheldon Selesnick & Franz G. Alexander, *The History of Psychiatry*, New York: Harper & Row, 1966 and *One Hundred Years of American Psychiatry*, published for the American Psychiatric Association by Columbia University Press, New York, 1944.
7. Fuller, Ibid., 1950.
8. S. Weir Mitchell. Proceedings of the American Medico-Psychological Association, 1:108, 1894.
9. Thirteenth Annual Report of the Trustees of Westboro Insane Hospital for the year ending September 30, 1897. Public Document No. 30, Wright & Potter Printing Co., Boston, MA, p. 16.
10. M. Kaplan and A. R. Henderson, Solomon Carter Fuller, M.D. (1872-1953): American pioneer in Alzheimer's disease research, in *The Journal of the History of the Neurosciences*, 2000, 9(3), p. 252.
11. Fuller, Ibid., 1950
12. Ibid., 1950.
13. Ibid., 1950
14. Fourteenth Annual Report of the Trustees of Westboro Insane Hospital for the year ending 1898. Public Document No. 30, Wright & Potter Printing Co., Boston, Mass., pp. 13, 20–25.
15. Fuller, Ibid., 1950.
16. Ibid., 1950.

17. Fourteenth Annual Report of the Trustees of Westboro Insane Hospital, 1898, Ibid., p. 25.

18. Paul Starr, *The Social Transformation of American Medicine*. New York: Basic Books, Inc., 1982, p. 112.

19. Established as *The Association of Medical Superintendents of American Institutions for the Insane* in 1892, *The American Medico-Psychological Association* later became *The American Psychiatric Association*.

20. Hurd, Ibid., p. 58.

21. Fuller, Ibid., 1950.

22. Ibid., 1950

23. From Solomon Carter Fuller's speech to the Livingstone College graduating class of 1943, upon acceptance of an honorary degree fifty years after his own graduation from the college.

24. For further reading on the development of research in neuropathology in the United States and Europe, see S. Flexner and J.T. Flexner, *William Henry Welch and the Heroic Age of American Medicine*, New York: Viking Press, 1941; E. Long, *A History of American Pathology*, Springfield, IL: C. Thomas, 1962; and G. Corner, *A History of the Rockefeller Institute, 1901-1953*, New York: Rockefeller Institute Press, 1964.

25. Sixteenth Annual Report of the Trustees of Westboro Insane Hospital for the year ending September 30, 1900. Public Document No. 30, Wright & Potter Printing Co., Boston, MA, p. 16.

26. Eighteenth Annual Report of the Trustees of Westboro Insane Hospital for the year ending September 30, 1902. Public Document No. 30, Wright & Potter Printing Co., Boston, MA, p. 18.

27. Editorial, Does it pay to be a Doctor?, *Journal of the American Medical Association*, 1904, 42, p. 247.

28. Minutes of the Board of Trustees of Westboro Insane Hospital, 1901, 1904.

29. *The Wisdom of Solomon*, unpublished report on Solomon Carter Fuller. The Solomon Carter Fuller Mental Health Center, Boston University.

30. S. C. Fuller, Jr. Interview, 1998.

31. L. Emmett Holt, A sketch of the development of the Rockefeller Institute for Medical Research, *Science*, July 1906, p. 1.

32. I. Gladston, Research in the United States. *Ciba Symposium*, 1946, 8, p. 362.

33. Letter to Solomon Carter Fuller from E. Lindon Mellis, Baltimore, April 20, 1904.

34. Minutes of the Board of Trustees, Westboro Insane Hospital, April 1904.

35. Minutes of the Board of Trustees, Westboro Insane Hospital, October 1904.

Chapter 5. The Science of Germany: Munich, 1904

1. F. T. Bonner. *American Doctors and German Universities*. Lincoln, NE: University of Nebraska Press, 1963.

2. Transcript of interview with Solomon Carter Fuller, 1951.

3. Ibid.

4. Ibid.

5. For further reading on the development of medical science in Germany in the late nineteenth and early twentieth centuries, see Henry Pachter, *Modern*

Germany, Boulder, CO: Westview Press, 1987; W. F. Bynum & R. Porter (Eds.), *Encyclopedia of the History of Medicine*, New York: Routledge, 1993; Thomas N. Bonner, *American Doctors and German Universities*, Lincoln, NE: University of Nebraska Press, 1963; Erwin Ackerknecht, *A Short History of Medicine*. New York: The Ronald Press Co., 1955.

6. Fuller, Ibid., 1951.
7. H. Hippius, G. Peters, D. Ploog, *Emil Kraepelin Memoirs*. Berlin/Heidelberg: Springer-Verlag, 1987, p. 68
8. Fuller. Ibid., 1951.
9. Ibid., 1951.
10. G. Perusini, Uber klinisch und histologischeh eigenartige psychische Erkankungen des spateren Lebensalter. In: F. Nissi, A. Alzheimer (eds.), *Histologische und Histopathologische Arbeiten*, vol. 3, Jena: Gustav Fisher, 1910, pp. 297-351. (English translation: K.L. Bick, L. Amaducci, G. Pepeu (eds.), *The Early Story of Alzheimer's Disease*, Padova: Liviana Press, 1987.)
11. M. Kaplan & A. R. Henderson, Solomon Carter Fuller, M.D. (1872-1953): American pioneer in Alzheimer's disease research. *Journal of the History of the Neurosciences*, vol. 9 (3), 2000, pp. 250-61.
12. Fuller, Ibid., 1951.
13. Lewy came to the United States after World War I and accepted the position of Visiting Professor of Neurophysiology at the University of Pennsylvania Medical School. See: Association for Research in Nervous and Mental Diseases. *Membership Directory*, 1942, p. 715.
14. For further reading on Auguste D., see S. Finger, *Origins of Neuroscience*, New York: Oxford University Press, 1994, pp. 351-52; K. Bick, The Early Story of Alzheimer's Disease. In R.D. Terry, R. Katzman, K. Bick, eds. *Alzheimer's Disease*. New York: Raven Press, 1994, pp. 1-8; and G.E. Berrios, Alzheimer's disease: a conceptual history. *International Journal of Geriatric Psychiatry,* 1987, pp. 355-65.
15. K. Maurer, S. Volk, H. Gerbaldo. Auguste D and Alzheimer's disease. *The Lancet*, vol. 349, 1997, pp. 1546-1549.
16. Kraepelin, *Psychiatrie*.8.Aufl. Barth, Leipzig, 1913.
17. G. W. Kreutzberg & W. Gudden. Alois Alzheimer. *Trends in Neuroscience*, vol. 11, pp. 256-57.
18. Fuller, Ibid., 1951.
19. Ibid.
20. S. C. Fuller's notes. 1950.

Chapter 6. The Doctor and the Sculptor: Westboro, 1906

1. Twenty-first Annual Report of the Trustees of Westboro Insane Hospital for the year ending September 30, 1905. Public Document No. 30, Wright & Potter Printing Co., Boston, MA, p. 16.
2. Ibid., p. 17.
3. The "Talented Tenth" consisted of several hundred urban, northern African American professionals, who were born between 1855 and 1875 and who came from affluent or privileged families. The term was created in 1896 by Henry L. Morehouse, a patron of liberal arts study for blacks, and was used to refer to a class of highly educated and moral African Americans that he hoped were

destined to be leaders and role models for blacks. For further reading on the "Talented Tenth", see D.L. Lewis, *W.E.B. DuBois: Biography of a Race*. New York: Henry Holt & Co., 1993 and W.E.B. DuBois, "The Talented Tenth", in J. Lester (Ed.), *The Seventh Son: The Thought and Writing of W.E.B. DuBois*, vol. 1, New York: Vintage Books, 1971.

4. S. G. Dannett. "Meta Vaux Warrick Fuller" *Profiles of Negro Womanhood*. Vol. 2: 20th Century, Yonkers, NY: Educational Heritage, 1966, pp. 30-46. The information presented in this publication was based on the author's interview with Meta Fuller in 1964.

5. W.E.B. DuBois, *The Philadelphia Negro*. Philadelphia: The University of Pennsylvania Press, 1996, p. 33.

6. S. G. Dannett. Ibid., p.32.

7. V. Hoover, Meta Vaux Warrick Fuller: Her life and art. *Negro History Bulletin*, 1977, vol. 40 (2): pp. 678-81.

8. S. G. Dannett, Ibid., p. 33.

9. Ibid., p. 35.

10. C. Hine (Ed.). *Black Women in America*. New York: Facts on File, 1997, p. 190.

11. V. Hoover, Ibid., p. 678.

12. S. G. Dannett, Ibid., p. 36.

13. Ibid., p. 36.

14. Ibid., p. 37.

Chapter 7. Pioneer in American Psychiatry: Framingham, 1909

1. L. O. Graham. *Member of the Club*. New York: Harper Collins, 1995, p. xiii.

2. A description of Framingham's 1900 Bicentennial Parade includes the mention of "coal black band playing and singing real coon songs to the delight of everyone". S. Herring, *Framingham: An American Town*. Framingham, MA: Framingham Historical Society and Framingham Tercentennial Commission, 2000, p. 237.

3. S. G. Dannett. "Meta Vaux Warrick Fuller" *Profiles of Negro Womanhood*. Vol. 2: 20th Century, Yonkers, NY: Educational Heritage, 1966, p. 37.

4. Ibid., p. 38.

5. For additional information on the "Boston School" of psychology, see G. Gifford (Ed.), *Psychoanalysis, Psychotherapy and the New England Medical Scene, 1894-1944*. New York: Science History Publications, 1978.

6. Solomon Carter Fuller's notes, 1950.

7. Ibid.

8. W. Forma. *They were Ragtime*. New York: Grosset & Dunlap, 1976, p. 153.

9. S. Freud. *An Autobiographical Study*. Translation by J. Strachey. New York: Norton & Co., 1952, p. 99.

10. Fuller, Ibid.

11. Karl M. Bowman, President of the American Psychiatric Association (1944-1946). From C. Prudhomme & D.F. Musto. *Historical Perspectives on Mental Health and Racism in the United States*. Paper presented at the Conference on Mental Health and Racism, Syracuse University, April 1971.

12. American Psychiatric Association, *One Hundred Years of American Psychiatry*. New York: Columbia University Press, 1944. Note: Massachusetts' Voluntary Admission Law (1895) provided that any person desiring admission to a hospital for the insane for the purpose of treatment could be admitted at his/her own request, if mentally competent to understand the nature of the admission. The law also stated that no voluntary patient could be detained longer than three days after giving notice that he/she desires to be discharged. In a study of temporary care admissions in Massachusetts' hospitals for the insane for the year 1912, Westborough was found to have a total of one hundred five, with fifty-eight of those admitted as voluntary patients. From Frankwood E. Williams, Legislation for the Insane in Massachusetts with Particular Reference to the Voluntary and Temporary Care Laws, *Boston Medical and Surgical Journal*, CLXXLLL (20), November 11, 1915, pp. 24-25.

13. H. M. Hurd (Ed.). *Mental Illness and Social Policy, Vol. II.* (Reprint of *The Institutional Care of the Insane in the United States and Canada*, 1916-1917 edition published by Johns Hopkins Press), New York: Arno Press, 1973, pp. 718–24. The concept of "Therapeutic Community" was developed by Maxwell Jones at the Dingleton Hospital in Melrose, Scotland. See M. Jones, *Therapeutic Community*. New York: Basic Books, Inc., 1953, p. 53.

14. S. C. Fuller, Jr. interview, 1998.

15. R. Hayden, *Eleven African American Doctors*. New York: Twenty-first Century Books, 1992, pp. 27, 28.

16. S. Dannett, Ibid., p. 38.

Chapter 8. Contributions to Science and Medicine: Westborough, 1911

1. S. C. Fuller, Jr., 1999.

2. Solomon Carter Fuller's notes, 1950.

3. Ibid.

4. S. C. Fuller, A study of the neurofibrils of demented paralytic, demented senilis, chronic alcoholics, cerebro lues and microcephalics. *American Journal of Insanity*, 1907, 63: 415.

5. S. C. Fuller's notes, Ibid.

6. E. Kraepelin, *Psychietrie: Ein Lehrbuch fur Studierende und Artze*. Verlag V. Johann Ambrosius Barth, 1910.

7. A. Alzheimer. Uber eigenartige Krankheitsfalle des spateren Alters. *Zeitschrift fur die gesamie Neurologie und Psychiatrie*. 1911, 4, pp. 356-85.

8. Fuller, Ibid.

9. S. C. Fuller. A study of the miliary plaques found in brains of the aged. *American Journal of Insanity*, 1911, 68:2, pp. 147–219.

10. S. C. Fuller. Alzheimer's disease (Senium Praecox). The report of a case and review of published cases. *Journal of Nervous and Mental Disease.* 1912, 36:44, pp. 440-55, 536–57.

11. M. Kaplan, & A. R. Henderson, Solomon Carter Fuller, M.D. (1872-1953): American pioneer in Alzheimer's disease research. *Journal of the History of the Neurosciences*. 2000, 9:3, pp. 250–61.

12. S. C. Fuller & H. L. Klopp. Further observations on Alzheimer's disease. *American Journal of Insanity*, 1912, 69 (1), pp.17–29.

13. V. Hoover. Meta Vaux Warrick Fuller: Her Life and Art. *Negro History Bulletin*. 1977, 40: 2, p. 679.
14. H.M. Hurd, (Ed.) *Mental Illness and Social Policy, Vol. II*. (Reprint of *The Institutional Care of the Insane in the United States and Canada*, 1916–1917 edition published by Johns Hopkins Press.), New York: Arno Press, Inc., 1973, p.723.
15. In 1910, there were 3409 Negro physicians in the United States – 2.5% of all physicians. From H. M. Morais. *The History of the Negro in Medicine*. The Association for the Study of Negro Life and History. New York: Publishers Co., 1967, p. 86.
16. S. C. Fuller, Jr., 1999.
17. S. W. Herring. *Framingham: An American Town*. Framingham, MA: The Framingham Historical Society, 2000, p. 265.
18. J. H. Franklin. *From Slavery to Freedom*. New York: Alfred Knopf, 1967, chapters 24, 25.
19. Fuller's files. Shortly after Woodrow Wilson's 1913 inauguration, southern cabinet officers proceeded with an executive order to purge the federal government workforce of African Americans and pushed for the elimination of commissions for nonwhites in the armed services. For additional reading on racial segregation during the Wilson presidency, see A. S. Link, *Woodrow Wilson and the Progressive Era: 1910-1917*. New York: Harper & Bros., 1954.
20. Fuller, Ibid.
21. S. G. L. Dannett. *Profiles of Negro Womanhood: Volume II, 20th Century*. The Negro Heritage Library. Yonkers, NY: Educational Heritage, Inc. 1966, p. 38.
22. Fuller, Jr., Ibid.
23. S. C. Fuller, Jr. In J. Graves, "Gladly Would He Learn and Gladly Teach." *Bostonia*, Fall 1995, p. 24.
24. Fuller, Jr., Ibid.
25. Fuller, Jr., Ibid.
26. K. N. Allen. *On the Beaten Path*. Littleton, NH: Sherwin/Dodge Printers, 1984, p. 336.
27. For additional information on the history of the Tuskegee Veterans Hospital, see W. H. Watson, *Against the Odds: Blacks in the Profession of Medicine in the United States*. New Brunswick, NJ: Transaction Publishers 1999; H. Morais, *The History of the Negro in Medicine*. The Association for the Study of Negro Life and History. New York: Publishers Co. 1967; and L. T. Wright, The Negro Physician. *The Crisis*, XXXVI, September, 1929, pp. 305–6.
28. Fuller, Ibid.
29. R. Sharpley. Solomon Carter Fuller. *Psychoanalysis, Psychotherapy and the New England Medical Scene, 1894-1944*. (George E. Gifford, Jr., ed.) New York: Science History Publications, 1978.
30. Wright., Ibid.
31. Fuller's files.

Chapter 9. The Later Years: Framingham, 1933

1. H. R. Isaacs. *The New World of Negro Americans*. New York: The John Day Co., 1965, p. 177.

2. S. C. Fuller in R. C. Hayden, *Eleven African American Doctors*. Frederick, MD: Twenty-First Century Books, 1992, p. 35.
3. In 1934, fewer than 150 black physicians were members of the American Medical Association and fifty of those were in New York City. From C. G. Woodson, *The Negro Professional Man and the Community*. Washington, DC: The Association for the Study of Negro Life and History, Inc., 1934, p. 119.
4. S. C. Fuller, Jr. interview, 1997.
5. Ibid.
6. S. C. Fuller, Jr. interview, 1999.
7. Ibid.
8. S. G. L. Dannett. "Meta Vaux Warrick Fuller", *Profiles of Negro Womanhood, Vol. 2, 20ᵗʰ Century*. Yonkers, NY: Educational Heritage, Inc., 1966, p. 40.
9. Ibid., p. 41.
10. S. C. Fuller files.
11. J. Ciment, "The Idea of Liberia". *American Legacy*, Fall 1998, 4 (3), pp. 32–42.
12. R. Weston Ballou interview, 2002.
13. Hayden, Ibid., p. 32.
14. S. C. Fuller, Jr. in J. Graves, "Dr. Solomon Carter Fuller (BUSM 1897): Gladly would he learn and gladly teach." *Bostonia*. Boston: Boston University, Fall 1995, 22–25.
15. S. C. Fuller, Jr. interview, 1999.
16. Ballou, Ibid.
17. Fuller, Jr., Ibid.
18. Ballou, Ibid.
19. J. L. Fuller interview, 2001.
20. Fuller, Jr., Ibid.
21. O. J. McNamara. "Solomon Carter Fuller," *Centerscope*. Boston: Boston University School of Medicine, Winter 1976, pp. 26-30.
22. Hayden., Ibid.
23. W. M. Cobb, "Dr. Solomon Carter Fuller: 1872-1953." *The Journal of the National Medical Association*, 1933, 46 (5), pp. 370-71.
24. The term "shell shock" was first used in 1915 by Charles Myers to describe three soldiers with symptoms of sleeplessness, reduced visual fields and amnesia following exposure to artillery shell explosions. From C. M. Myers, "Contributions to the study of shell shock." *Lancet*, February 1915, 13, pp. 316–320. See also, A. Deutsch, "Military psychiatry", *One Hundred Years of American Psychiatry*, New York: Columbia University Press, 1947, pp. 433-34.
25. H. R. Isaacs. *The New World of Negro Americans*. New York: The John Day Co., 1963.
26. Cobb, Ibid.
27. Dannett, Ibid., pp. 44-45.
28. V. J. Hoover. "Meta Vaux Warrick Fuller: Her life and art." *Negro History Bulletin*, March–April 1977, 40 (2), p. 681.

Chapter 10. Recognition of Accomplishments: Boston, 1974

1. S.C. Fuller's file, date unknown.
2. O. J. McNamara. "Solomon Carter Fuller." *Centerscope*. Boston: Boston University School of Medicine, Winter 1976, pp. 26-30.

3. E. Pinderhughes interview, 2001.
4. P. Staff. *The Social Transformation of American Medicine.* New York: Basic Books, 1982, pp. 337, 339.
5. M. A. Neumann & R. Cohn. "Incidence of Alzheimer's disease in a large mental hospital: Relation to senile psychosis and psychosis with cerebral arteriosclerosis." *Archives of Neurology & Psychiatry* 1953, 69, pp.615-36. For additional reading on the early contributions to Alzheimer's research, see K.L. Bick, "The early story of Alzheimer disease." In R. D. Terry, R. Katzman, & K. L. Bick, (Eds.). *Alzheimer Disease.* Philadelphia: Lippincott-Raven Publishers, 1994, pp. 1-8.
6. S. C. Fuller, Jr., 1999.
7. B. Carney. "Family gathers as Framingham dedicates Fuller Middle School." *Middlesex News*, Framingham, April 3, 1995, pp. 1A, 8A.

Epilogue: Washington, D.C., 2001

1. H. Fuller interview, 2003.
2. S. C. Fuller. In a letter to Luther P. Jackson, Virginia State College, Petersburg, Virginia, March 27, 1950.

Index

Aborigines (Liberia), 11-12
Academie Colarossi, 45
Acley, Miss, 44-45
Adams, George, 21-22, 25
Adler, Alfred, 52, 60
Allentown State Hospital
    (Pennsylvania), 53, 73
Alzheimer, Alois, 35, 36-38, 50, 56-58
American Art Student's Club for
    Women (Paris), 44-45
American Colonization Society (ACS),
    4-5, 7, 12
American Girl's Club. *See* American
    Art Student's Club for Women
    (Paris)
American Medical Association, 68, 75
American Medico-Psychological
    Association, 22, 26-27
American Methodist Episcopal Church,
    15, 17
American Psychiatric Association, 65,
    80
American Society for Colonizing Free
    People of Color in the United
    States. *See* American
    Colonization Society (ACS)
Americo-Liberians, 11-12
Angelou, Maya, vii
Ashmun, Jehudi, 7-8
Atlantic City, 27, 43, 47
Auguste D., 37

Ayer, James, 76
Baker, Dr., 25
Baltimore, 8
Barclay, Arthur, 33, 70
Barclay, Sara, 33
Belding, 56
Belleview Hospital Medical College,
    28
Bent, Arthur, 50
Betts, 57
Biggs, Hermann, 28
Bing, Samuel, 46
Bioko, Equatorial Guinea. *See*
    Fernando Po
Black Psychiatrists of America, 80
Blocq, 57
Board of Donations for Education
    (Liberia), 18-19
Bollinger, Otto, 35
Boston Medical Center, vii
Boston Psychopathic Hospital, 18
Boston Stock Exchange, 69
Boston Symphony, 63
Boston University, 27
Boston University Division of
    Psychiatry, 80
Boston University Medical Center, 79
Boston University School of Medicine,
    18, 21, 26, 29, 41, 53, 64, 65, 67-
    68, 80
Boundary Commission of Liberia, 11

Boy Scouts of America, 69
Bragg, Evan, 29
Bragg, Mary (May). *See* Weston, Mary
    (May) Bragg
Branche, George, 65
Brooklyn, New York, 48
Brown, Auntie, 50
Brown, Margaret, 47
Brown, Nancy, 5
Brush, Edward, 52
Burleigh, Harry, 63
Calderon, Pablo, 81
Caldwell (Liberia), 12
Calloway, Thomas, 45
Campbell, Macfie, 65
Carles, Antoine, 45
Carnegie Institute, 28
Cartier, Alexander, 47
cassada, 9
Catskill Mountains, New York, 17
Charitable Mechanics Society (Boston),
    9
Clark Celebration, 51
Clark University (Worcester,
    Massachusetts), 50-52
Clarke, 57
Clay, Henry, 4
Clinical Society Commission of
    Massachusetts, 26
Colby College, 68, 74
Colby, Edward P., 21-22
Coles, Dr., 31
College Preparatory School
    (Monrovia), 13
Collin, Raphael, 45
Colored Episcopal Church, Atlantic
    City, 47
Congoes, 11
Councilman, W.T., 39, 55-56
cran-cran, 9
Crane, Stephen, 46
Crisis, The, 59, 65
Cushing, Harvey, 53
Cushing Hospital (Framingham), 77
Davis, Harvey, 65
Deaver, Rev. Mr., 47
Democratic Party, 75
Dr. Solomon Carter Fuller Mental
    Health Center, vii-viii, 79-80
DuBois, W.E.B., 42, 58-59, 62

Dunford, Judith, 1
Dunham, Edward K., 28, 36, 38
Earhart, Amelia, 70
Ecole des Beaux Arts, 45
Edinger, Ludwig, 38
Ehrlich, Paul, 38-40, 55
Eisenhower, Dwight, 75
Elizabeth, New Jersey, 69
Ellison, Ralph, ix
Elmwood Opera House (Framingham),
    49
Emancipation Proclamation, 59
Episcopal Church, Atlantic City, 47
Equal Suffrage Movement, 70
Ethiopia Awakening, 46
Fair Employment Practices
    Commission, 75
Fay, Harold, 63
Ferenczi, Sandor, 51
Fernando Po, 71
Firestone Company, 11, 71
Fischer, 57
Fisk Jubilee Singers, 44
Framingham Dramatic Club, 63
Framingham, Massachusetts, 49-50, 54,
    72, 76, 77, 81
Framingham South High School. *See*
    Fuller Middle School
Framingham's Women's Club, 77
Framingham Union Hospital, 76
Frankfort, Germany, 38-40
Freud, Sigmund, 50, 51, 60
Fuller, Anna Ursula James, 10-11, 33,
    71
Fuller, Harriet, 83-84
Fuller, Henry, 3, 10
Fuller, John Lewis (grandfather of
    SCF), xiv, 1-5, 7-10, 84
Fuller, John Lewis (grandson of SCF),
    xv, 73-74
Fuller, John Lewis Jr., 3
Fuller, Margaret, 3
Fuller, Meta Vaux Warrick. *See*
    Warrick, Meta Vaux
Fuller Middle School, 81
Fuller, Nancy (daughter of John Lewis
    Fuller). *See* Jarratt, Nancy Fuller
Fuller, Nancy (wife of John Lewis
    Fuller), 2-3, 5
Fuller, Perry James, 62, 68-70

Fuller, Rebecca, 3, 8

Fuller, Sarah, 3, 5

Fuller, Solomon (father of SCF), 3, 5, 8, 10-14

Fuller, Solomon Carter: birth, 10; education in Liberia, 12-14; education at Livingstone College, North Carolina, 15-17; education at Boston University, 18-21; internship at Westboro Insane Hospital, 22-24; pathologist at Westboro, 24-31; post-graduate education in Munich, xiii-xv, 30-38; visit to Frankfort, 38-40; pathologist at Westboro (after visit to Germany), 41-42, 55-56; early relationship with and marriage to Meta Vaux Warrick, 42, 46-48; home and visitors in Framingham, 49-50, 62-63; research and publication, 56-58, 59; psychiatric practice, 60; military and veteran-related activities, 60-62, 64-65, 75; attitudes toward wife's art career, 62, 76; retirement from Boston University, 67-68; relationship to his sons, 63, 68-69; relationship to family in Liberia, 70-71; visits by Liberians, 71; religious beliefs, 71-72; friends in later years, 72-73; blindness and old age, 73-75; death and funeral services, 76

Fuller, Solomon Carter Jr., x, xiv-xv, 53-55 passim, 60-63 passim, 68-69, 72-76 passim, 79, 81 passim

Fuller, Thomas (uncle of SCF), 3, 5, 10

Fuller, Thomas George (brother of SCF), 11, 70-71

Fuller, William Thomas (Tom), 58, 68-69, 73, 76

Gibraltar, 33-34

Gibson, 13

Goldman, Emma, 51

Gorman Theatre (Framingham), 49

Grace Church (Framingham), 70

Graham, Lawrence Otis, 49

Greenwich Village, 69

Haines, Thomas, 13

Hall, G. Stanley, 50-51

Harding Administration, 64

Harlem, 69

Harnack, Adolf von, 34

Harriet Tubman Square Park, 59

Harvard Medical School, 39, 55-56, 66, 72, 80

Hayden Scholarship, 18

Hayes, Roland, 63

Hemings, Fred, 47

Hemings, Sally, 10, 47

Henderson, Alfred R, ix-x

Herter, Christian A., 28

Hilton, Frances, 13

Hines, General, 65

Hinton, William, 72

Hodes, J. Allison, 26

Hodge, Professor, 51

Holt, L. Emmett, 30

Hoover, Velma, 59

Hospital for Sick and Injured Colored War Veterans. See Tuskegee Veterans Hospital

Howard University, 76

Hurd, Henry Mills, 52

Imperial Institute for Chemical Research, Frankfort, 38

Isaacs, Harold R., 67

James, Anna Ursula. See Fuller, Anna Ursula James

James, Benjamin Van Rensalaer, 10-11

James, Commodore, 10

James, William, 53

Jamestown Tercentennial Exposition, 46-47

Jansen, 58

Jarratt, Alexander, 2-3

Jarratt family, 17, 48

Jarratt, Nancy Fuller, 2-3

jiggers, 9

J. Liberty Tadd (Philadelphia art school), 44

Johann Wolfgang Goethe University, 37

Johns Hopkins Medical School, 24, 28, 30, 52

Johnson, Elijah, 7

Johnson, Simon, 65

Jones, Emma. See Warrick, Emma Jones.

Jones, Henry, 43

Joslin Diabetes Center (Boston), 73
Jung, Carl, 51, 52, 60
Keene, New Hampshire, 72-73
Kennedy School of Government
    (Harvard University), 83
King, Charles D.B., 71
King, Charles H., Jr., 21
King, Drue, 65
Klopp, Henry, 28, 53
Knight, E.G., 47
Koch, Robert, 28
Kraepelin, Emil, xiii, 30, 35, 38, 41, 50,
    52, 57
Ku Klux Klan, 60
Lafora, 58
Larner's Pond, 70
L'Art Nouveau (Parisian art salon), 46
Lewy, Frederich H., 37
Liberia, 5, 7-14, 18-19, 33, 70-71. *See
    also* Monrovia, Liberia
Liberia College, 13-14
Livingstone College (Salisbury, NC),
    15-17, 75, 77
Long Branch, New Jersey, 17
Long Island College Hospital, 17-18
Loudin, Frederick, 44
Loudin, Harriet, 44
Mahl, Professor, 24
Mallory, 56, 57-58
Man Eating His Heart, 46, 54
Manhattan Beach Hotel, 18
Marlboro Hospital (Framingham), 53,
    73
Martha's Vineyard Sound, 76, 77
Maryland (Liberia), 10. 11
Mary Turner, 46
Massachusetts Clinical Society
    Commission, 53
Massachusetts Department of Mental
    Health, v
Massachusetts Legislature, 79
Massachusetts Memorial Hospital, 53,
    64
Massachusetts State Board of Insanity,
    52
Massachusetts State Hospital for the
    Insane. *See* Westborough State
    Hospital
Max Planck Institute of Psychiatry, 35

Mechanics Charitable Society
    (Monrovia), 9
Mellis, Edward, 22, 23-24, 30
Menninger Clinic, 66
Menninger, Karl, 66
Merriam, John, 49
Merrill Lynch, 69
Meyer, Adolf, 50, 52, 53
Middlesex County Sanitarium, 76
Mitchell, S. Weir, 22-23
Monroe, James, 7
Monrovia, Liberia, 5, 7, 33, 70. *See
    also* Liberia
Mt. Moriah Cemetery, Philadelphia, 43
Munich Psychiatric Hospital, 35
Murray Hill Hotel, New York, 17
National Association for the
    Advancement of Colored People
    (NAACP), 58-59, 64, 75, 77
National Medical Association, 64, 80
New England Medical Gazette, 29
Newport, Rhode Island, 64
Newport Yacht Club, 10, 64
"New Vistas in American Art"
    exhibition, 76
New York City, 28, 70
New York University School of
    Medicine, 28
Niagara Movement, 42
Nimmo (or Nimo), Rebecca, 5, 13
Norfolk, Virginia, 1-5
North Carolina, 15-17
Overholser, Winfred, 65-66
Page, Naida Willette, 80
Paris Exposition of 1899, 45
Paris Exposition of 1900, 45
Peace Halting the Ruthlessness of War,
    62
Pennsylvania College of Art. *See*
    Philadelphia School of Industrial
    Art
Pentagon, 83
Peter Brent Brigham Hospital (Boston),
    53
Petersburg, Virginia, 1-2
Philadelphia, 43-44, 54, 69
Philadelphia Academy of Fine Arts, 44
Philadelphia Academy of Music, 43
Philadelphia School of Industrial Art,
    44

Pierce, Pr., 10
Pinderhughes, Charles, 74, 80
Plaut, Felix, 35
Price, Joseph Charles, 16
Price Memorial Building (Livingstone
    College), 75
Procession of Arts and Crafts, The, 44
Prudhomme, Charles, 80
Psychiatric Hospital (Boston), 65
Randolph, A. Philip, 75
"Red Summer" (1919), 60
Reid, Mrs. Whitelaw, 45
Reiss, Edward, 35
Roberts, Joseph Jenkins, 7, 8
Robeson, Paul, 63
Rockefeller Institute, 28, 30
Rodin, Auguste, 46
Rodriguez, Juan, 81
Roosevelt, Franklin, 65, 75
Roosevelt, Theodore, 47
Saint-Gaudens, Augustus, 45
Schmaus, Hans, 35-36
Senckenberg Institute, 38
September 11, 2001 attack on
    Pentagon, 83
Sharply, Robert H., 80
Sheepshead Bay, 18
Sherbrook, 7
Shredded Wheat Company, 47
Sidney, Maine, 29
Sierra Leone, 7, 11
Sierra Leone Mountains, 34
sleeping disease, 9
"Solomon Carter Fuller Day", 80
Solomon Fuller Institute, 80
Sousa, John Philip, 18
Southard, Elmer, 18, 56
South-West German Alienists, 37
Southwest German Psychiatric Society,
    57
Spirit of Emancipation, 59
St. Andrew's Episcopal Church
    (Framingham), 77
Stanley, Robert C., 64
Star of Zion, 17
State Reform School for Boys
    (Massachusetts), 21
St. Elizabeth's Psychiatric Hospital
    (Washington, DC), 65
Stewart, Margaret, 10-11

St. Stephen's Church (Framingham), 60
St. Thomas Church (Philadelphia), 47
Submarine Signal Company, 63
Supreme Court, 75
Sutherland, John P., 25, 65
Syphilis and Its Treatment, 72
Talented Tenth, 42
Tanner, Henry O., 44-45
Tildon, Toussaint T., 65
Townsend, Rev. Mr., 47
Trent, William J., 77
Truman, Harry, 75
Tuskegee Air Base, 69
Tuskegee, Alabama, 64
Tuskegee Institute, 64
Tuskegee Veterans Hospital, 64-65
Tyzzer, Ernest, 39
United Community Services (Boston),
    69
United States Armed Forces, 64
United States Army, Secretary of, 83
United States Veterans' Bureau, 64-65
University of Munich, xi, 30, 35
Vaux, Richard, 43
Ventnor, New Jersey, 43
Veterans Administration. *See* United
    States Veterans' Bureau
Virchow, Rudolf, 22
Voit, Karl von, 35
von Harnack, Adolf. *See* Harnack,
    Adolf von
von Voit, Karl. *See* Voit, Karl von
Waller, Meta Louis Fuller, 83-84
Ward, Dr., 74
War Department, 61-62
Warren, President (Carnegie Institute),
    36
Warrick, Blanche, 44
Warrick, Emma Jones, 43, 44
Warrick, Meta Vaux: ancestry, birth,
    and early childhood, 43; art
    education in the United States, 44;
    postgraduate study in Paris, 44-46;
    friendship with W.E.B. DuBois,
    45-46; early relationship with and
    marriage to Solomon Carter
    Fuller, 42, 46-48; home in
    Framingham, 49-50, 54; birth of
    son Solomon Jr., 54; loss of
    artwork to fire, 54; birth of son

Tom, 58; return to art activities,
        58-59, 62-63, 70, 72, 76-77; birth
        of son Perry, 62; community,
        religious, and political activities,
        63, 70, 72, 76-77, 81; death, 77;
        bust of SCF, 79
Warrick, William H., 43, 44
Washington, Booker T., 16, 42
Webster, Thomas, 66
Weigert, Carl, 38
Weiler, Karl, 35
Welch, William Henry, 28
Westboro Insane Hospital. *See*
        Westborough State Hospital
Westborough (or Westboro) State
        Hospital Papers, 29, 59
Westborough State Hospital (originally
        Westboro Insane Hospital), 21-31,
        36, 52-53, 56, 59, 64, 73
Weston, Arthur, 72-73
Weston, Mary (May) Bragg, 29-30, 68,
        72-73, 76
Weston, Ruth, 72-73
West Virginia State College, 74
Williams, Frankwood E., 61-62
Women's Peace Party, 62, 70
Wood, Harry, 17
Worcester State Hospital, 50
World War I, 60-62, 64, 75
World War II, 75
Wretched, The, 54
Wright, Clarence W., 75
Wright, Louis T., 65
YMCA (Harlem), 69

About the Author

Mary Kaplan is a faculty member in the School of Aging Studies at the University of South Florida, where she teaches courses on Alzheimer's disease, mental health and aging, and geriatric case management. She received her master's degree in social work at Catholic University in Washington, D. C. and is a licensed clinical social worker. Ms. Kaplan has worked in the fields of gerontology and health care for 30 years as a direct care provider, administrator, and educator. She has published numerous books, articles, chapters, and training manuals on geriatric health and mental health care, case management, and dementia care.

Made in the USA
San Bernardino, CA
08 December 2013